Sundance to Sarajevo

Sundance to Sarajevo

Film Festivals and the World They Made

Kenneth Turan

UNIVERSITY OF CALIFORNIA PRESS

Berkeley   Los Angeles   London

University of California Press
Berkeley and Los Angeles, California

University of California Press, Ltd.
London, England

© 2002 by the Regents of the University of California

Library of Congress Cataloging-in-Publication Data

Turan, Kenneth.
  Sundance to Sarajevo : film festivals and the world they
made / Kenneth Turan.
      p.   cm.
  ISBN 0-520-21867-1 (alk. paper)
    1. Film festivals.   I. Title.

PN1993.4 .T865   2002
791.43'079 — dc21   2001044418

Manufactured in Canada
10   09   08   07   06   05   04   03   02
10   9   8   7   6   5   4   3   2   1

The paper used in this publication meets the minimum
requirements of ANSI/NISO Z39.48-1992 (R 1997)
(*Permanence of Paper*). ⊛

To B, for everything, for always

CONTENTS

PART THREE:
FESTIVALS WITH AESTHETIC AGENDAS

PART FOUR:
THE POLITICS OF FESTIVALS

Acknowledgments

While a fiction writer can create on his or her own, a journalist, to para-phrase Tennessee Williams's especially apt line, is always depending on the kindness of strangers. And when a book has been in the works for as long as this one, close to a decade, that's an awful lot of thank yous.

I'd like to start with people who are hardly strangers, past and current staff at the *Los Angeles Times*, where earlier versions of many of these pieces appeared. Shelby Coffey III, Narda Zacchino, and John Lindsay made it possible for me to become the paper's film critic, and several lev-els of editors — Oscar Garza, Ann Hurley, Rich Nordwind, Kelly Scott, and Sherry Stern — supported my passion for watching films in distant lands. Francine Della Catena and Cindy Hively helped with selecting and procuring photographs, and *Calendar*'s fine copy editors, too numer-ous to mention, had the unenviable task of trying to keep errors out of my stories. I'd also like to thank the editors of *Smithsonian*, where a different version of the Pordenone chapter appeared, for believing that the silent film revival was worth a trip to Italy to investigate.

At each festival I went to, the staff and fellow journalists who helped me are too numerous to single out individually, but I could never have survived without their cheerful, selfless assistance. Where Sundance and Cannes are concerned, because I've attended for more than ten years in a row, I'm going to break precedent and thank Sandra Sapperstein and R.J. Millard for the former and Catherine Verret and Christine Aimé for the latter. I also have nothing but gratitude for the owners and staffs of the Old Miners' Lodge in Park City, Utah, and the Hotel Splendid in Cannes, which have made me feel so at home that I look forward to staying at their establishments at least as much as to the festivals in question.

I'll always be grateful to James Clark at the University of California Press for immediately and wholeheartedly believing in this project, and to Eric Smoodin, who made the transition to finished book as smooth as possible. And of course my agent, Kathy Robbins, whose assistance with the contract was invaluable.

When film becomes your life, it's hard to have any other kind of life, and I would really be remiss if I didn't acknowledge the friends who put up with me while all this was going on. That also goes for my daughters, Whitney and Devin, who have enriched my life in unexpected ways. And to my wife Patty Williams, who also took many of the book's photographs, my thanks are too strong and complex to be safely entrusted to words.

Introduction

No one wants to speak against the Bible, but the sentiment found in Ecclesiastes famously insisting "to every thing there is a season, and a time to every purpose under heaven" in no way applies to the universe of film festivals.

Month in, month out, from the Flickfest International Outdoor Short Film Festival starting in early January in the Bondi Beach area of Sydney, Australia, through the Autrans Festival of Mountain and Adventure Films ending in mid-December in the high, thin air of southeast France, there is barely a day on the calendar where some film festival is not being celebrated in some exotic city somewhere in the world.

Haugesund, Norway, Oulu, Finland, and Umeå, Sweden, have festivals, as does Trencianske Teplice in the Slovak Republic, India's Thiruvananathapuram, Iran's Kish Island ("the Pearl of the Persian Gulf"), the Australian beach resort of Noosa, and the Italian city of Udine, which unexpectedly bills itself as "the world's largest showcase of popular East Asian cinema." There are nearly sixty Jewish film festivals in existence but only one QT event, in which director Quentin Tarantino annually takes over the Alamo Drafthouse Cinema in Austin, Texas, and shows favorite films to benefit the Austin Film Society. There is even an intentionally stateless movable feast called Transfest, which facilitates "the simple idea of introducing film festivals which take place somewhere in the world, in another place."

Festivals have become such a growth industry that Missoula, Montana, has two and a petite but trendy town like Telluride, Colorado, now has three (MountainFilm Festival and IndieFest 2K in addition to the regular Telluride event). And, especially in Europe, various coordinating bodies have grown up to try and create order out of the impending chaos.

On the largest scale, the European Coordination of Film Festivals, created to remedy "the disparity of practises and some dangerous excesses and trends" of the continent's proliferating fests, listed 76 festivals when it began in 1995, a number that had more than doubled to 154 in twenty countries by 2000. On a different note, the existence of overlapping science-fiction-oriented events led to the birth of a European Fantasy Film Festivals Federation to, in its own words, "put an end to a grubby war and sign an armistice." This group joins festivals in Porto, Brussels, Luxembourg, Rome, Espoo, Stiges, Amsterdam, Lund, and San Sebastián to, among other things, annually present the Méliès d'Or (named after the great French imaginative director), a.k.a. The Grand Prize of European Fantasy Film.

Even with all these official bodies, no one seems to be exactly sure how many festivals there are in the world, not even books created specifically to keep track of them. *The Variety Guide to Film Festivals* by Steven Gaydos lists more than four hundred, while three other books (*International Film Festival Guide* by Shael Stolberg, *The Film Festival Guide* by Adam Langer, and *The Ultimate Film Festival Survival Guide* by Chris Gore) record over five hundred each.

Because, except for big names like Cannes and Sundance, there is less overlap in these listings than one might expect, it's possible that an outlandish-sounding *New York Times* estimate of more than a thousand fests around the world might not be as wild as it seems. That's enough for the festival circuit to have its own print publication ("*Iff*, the international film festival magazine") as well as a DVD periodical called *Film-Fest*, which happily describes itself as "your exclusive all-access pass to the latest movies, the coolest parties, the hottest filmmakers and the brightest stars that travel the globe to celebrate the art of film."

Not surprisingly, film festivals are especially a growth area in the United States — so much so that critic David Thomson, in an arch list in *Movieline* magazine entitled "100 Questions We Honestly Want to Ask Hollywood" ("What is Tom Cruise going to do instead of aging?" "Why do they make the new James Bond films seem as if they were made in 1962?"), found space to wonder "Can anyone name five cities in America that do not now have film festivals?"

This proliferation is visible across the board. While New York, ever the cultural behemoth, hosts an estimated thirty festivals (the wildest being the New York Underground Film Festival, annually home to questionable items like *Home Brewer Serial Killer* and *Farley Mowat Ate My Brother*), North Carolina boasts thirteen, including something called the Hi Mom Film Festival in Chapel Hill.

It's one thing for just about every city within cheering distance of Los Angeles (Palm Beach, Malibu, Idyllwild, Temecula, San Luis Obispo, Santa Barbara, Santa Monica, Santa Clarita, the Silver Lake neighborhood proper, and the surfside trio of Newport Beach, Laguna Beach, and Hermosa Beach) to have a festival; it's another to witness a similar proliferation in the Midwest. Say hello to the Great Plains Film Festival in Lincoln, Nebraska, the Heartland Film Festival in Indianapolis, even the Hardacre Film Festival in wee Tipton, Iowa, set in the historic circa 1917 Deco-style Hardacre Theater and created, its promotional material would have you believe, to answer that age-old question, "Yes, but will it play in . . . Iowa?"

One result of this phenomenal growth is that films no one has heard of can take home heaps of honors. The yet-to-be-distributed and all-but-unseen *Wedding Cow* (formerly known as *Good Cows Are Hard to Find*) boasted in a press release of winning a full ten awards, including the Daedalos from IndieKINO, the International Independent Online Film Festival of Seoul, South Korea, and the Golden Unicorn from the

Europäisches Filmfestival Alpinale in Bludenz, Austria. Garry Trudeau astutely gave a nod to this fest-mania in his "Doonesbury" comic strip by having B.D.'s actress wife Boopsie, the star of "Chugalug," "Beer-blasters," and "Pompom Pam," be the subject of "The Barbara Ann Boopstein Film Festival," sponsored by the Aspen Ski Patrol and high-lighted by, she is pleased to report, "a panel discussion of my film work! Led by Roger Ebert!"

Even a Boopstein festival doesn't seem out of place when you con-sider some of the stranger names on the festival circuit, events so out-landish they sound apocryphal even if they're not. What is one to make of items with names like the Takoma Tortured Artists Film Festival in Washington State; Eat My Shorts! Comedy Short Film Showcase in Montreal, Canada; Eat My Schlock! Home Grown Trash Film Festival in Brisbane, Australia; and Short Attention Span Film and Video Festival in San Francisco — not to mention another San Francisco event, the Brainwash Movie Festival, whose top prize is said to be the "Charles Manson Loose Eyeball" award?

The first movie event I was exposed to growing up in Brooklyn was the always serious New York Film Festival, which began in 1963 and included in its first five years classics like Roman Polanski's *Knife in the Water*, Milos Forman's *Loves of a Blonde*, Gillo Pontecorvo's *The Battle of Algiers*, Bernardo Bertolucci's *Before the Revolution*, and an explosion of films from Jean-Luc Godard: *Band à Part, Une Femme Est une Femme, Alphaville*, and *Masculine-Feminine*.

Not that I had the means to actually see all these films; it's the feeling of festivity and potential I remember from my younger days, the excite-ment of the full-page ad announcing the event's selections, written up in stirring prose, that appeared every year, one time only, in exactly the same format in the Sunday Arts and Leisure section of the *New York Times*. I felt, as I have not always felt since, the sense of a door opening into a world of culture and sophistication I had no idea existed, as well as the hope that there might be a place in there for me.

That feeling was only part of what I experienced in 1971 during my first trip to a major world cinema event, representing the *Washington Post* at the Cannes Film Festival in the exotic (to me, at least) south of France. Mostly I was exhausted, deluged by more movies more often than I wanted to handle.

As naive as I was young, I confided these thoughts to the storied Italian director Luchino Visconti, one of the masters of cinema, who was doing interviews to promote his *Death in Venice*. "Isn't it a bit overwhelming?" I said to the great man, whose vibrant argyle socks I still remember. Visconti turned his hawklike, aristocratic face, features suitable for a fifteenth-century condotierre, to me in shock. "It is cinema, cinema, cinema, all the day long," he said, restating the obvious for my benefit. "I love it."

From that time to this, I have struggled to have Visconti's enthusiastic attitude toward festivals, but it has not been uniformly easy. Though they are often held in pleasant, diverting cities, too many theaters, too many deadliness, too large crowds, too much relentless hype, and too few memorable films can make these events more of an exasperating ordeal than might be imagined for a working reporter or critic.

Yet, paradoxically, it was the enormous number of cinematic celebrations overloading the world circuit that reinvigorated my interest in film festivals. I was intrigued by how many there were, how they styled themselves, and in what unexpected corners of the globe they appeared. I began acquiring brochures and pamphlets from events that caught my interest, and soon I had a collection serious enough, if not for a doctoral thesis, at least for some broad general observations.

Given that there are so many of them, the key thing these multiple festivals share is a need to differentiate themselves from each other. Sometimes the boast is straightforward, if a bit narrow, like Neuchâtel's claim to be "the only Swiss film festival devoted to the bizarre and the imagination," Toronto's Rendezvous with Madness and its focus on the myth and reality of mental illness, or the Rencontres Internationales Henri Langlois in Poitiers, France, which concentrates on film school projects, annually choosing some sixty examples from approximately three thousand short- and medium-length works nominated by 140 schools.

Sometimes a festival's unifying concept is completely unexpected. The Golden Knight Slavonic Film Festival in the Ukrainian city of Kiev focuses on Slav brotherhood and Orthodox Christian values. Copenhagen's Night Film Festival annually sells 40,000 tickets despite screening all its films between midnight and 6 A.M. while, at the opposite end of the spectrum, Italy's International Giffoni Children's Film Festival recruits kids to discuss films with their directors and stars.

Occasionally the fit between subject and locale is so good that the synergy creates an international institution. Dinard, a town in France's Brittany, became so identified with its Festival of British Cinema that it placed a giant replica of the event's trophy, director Alfred Hitchcock with a bird on each shoulder, on the local boardwalk. And Cognac's devotion to thrillers and suspense films means that festival guests are politely fingerprinted in the town square and get served brandy and orange juice cocktails before screenings. In the United States, both Nantucket ("Where Screenwriters Inherit the Earth") and Austin ("King of the Screenplay Festivals") have made names for themselves by focusing on the underappreciated writer, with the Texas festival handing out what it calls "the coveted (and lethally heavy) Austin Film Festival Typewriter Award."

Perhaps the oddest corner of the festival universe is the one for films that other events have scoffed at. Roger Ebert uses the University of Illinois at Urbana-Champaign to host an Overlooked Film Festival, and one of the several festivals at home in Santa Monica is called "Dances with Films" (motto "No Politics. No Stars. No Sh*t"), which insists its entries must have no known actors, producers, or directors or, for that matter, no money from any known company.

Most refreshingly forthright of these events is Philadelphia's baldly named Reject Film Festival, with a VCR reject button for its logo and a frank parenthetical slogan: "As if a gathering of bitter, angry artists could be called a 'festival.'" Proud of the way it "enables filmmakers to triumph in the face of rejection," it requires a dismissive letter from another event with its application and has become so popular, *Daily Variety* reports, that "the Reject Festival is not above rejection itself."

Besides coming up with surprising concepts, festivals can also set themselves apart by the nature of the prizes they give competitors. No two festivals hand out the same award, though after taking account of things like the Golden Raven (Brussels), the Golden Frog (Toruń, Poland), the Golden Calf (Utrecht), the Golden Olive (Kalamata, Greece), the Golden Orange (Antalya, Turkey), the Golden Bayard (Namur, France), the Golden Boomerang (Noosa), the Golden Alexander (Thessaloniki), and the Golden Anchor (Haifa), it does seem there is no object, either natural or man-made, that has not been gilded for presentation.

Perhaps tired of this particular gold rush, the Taos Talking Pictures Festival has gone in another direction with its top prize, the Taos Land Grant Award, which is nothing less than five acres of homestead property atop the Taos Mesa. The idea, the festival says, is "to plant media artists in the fertile soil of New Mexico" with the hope that a filmmaking community will take root and flower.

As to why so many festivals are flowering here and now, the reasons are severalfold, starting with the desire of the municipalities that host them to get their names before a wide public and attract visitors both during and after the celebration in question.

The key cause of festival proliferation, however, is a symbiotically linked trio of factors. Newly active independent and foreign-language filmmakers hunger for appreciative audiences, a need that dovetails nicely with audience members' yearning for alternatives to the standard Hollywood fare that dominates film screens not only in this country but also worldwide. And small distributors as well as national film industries locked into an unequal battle with the American juggernaut see these hungers as a not-to-be-missed opportunity to both earn money and promote their goods to the fullest extent.

For while movie fans have not lost their taste for the artistic and noncommercial, theaters are not always willing to risk showing those films. "Of course there are too many festivals," Pierre-Henri Deleau, former head of Cannes's Directors Fortnight told *Daily Variety*. "People are going to them because theaters aren't doing their jobs to show films from the rest of the world."

Festivals have become, in effect, what Piers Handling, head of the powerful Toronto Film Festival, has called "an alternative distribution network. A lot of work only gets shown now at festivals. A lot of foreign-language film that would get distribution ten years ago doesn't get seen anymore." France has been especially assiduous in using festivals around the world to get its cinema seen, and it's impossible to imagine the current critical rage for Iranian films without the intense exposure these works have gotten at Cannes, New York, and elsewhere.

Even for those films that do get seen outside festivals, the event and its high-profile gathering of critics and journalists as well as the kind of intense partisans who create word of mouth mean festivals are also useful to distributors as an inexpensive marketing tool for about-to-be-released movies that can't afford to lavish tens of millions of dollars on print and television advertising.

"We'll play every regional festival we can," Tom Bernard of Sony Pictures Classics told the *New York Times*. "It's all about building buzz and creating awareness. Film festivals are an alternate p.r. universe. They save us millions." And earn millions as well. A key to the unprecedented success of Sony's *Crouching Tiger, Hidden Dragon* (four Oscars and more than $100 million at the box office, a U.S. record for a subtitled picture) was its shrewd use of film festival exposure, starting with a rapturous world premier at Cannes, a brief stop at Telluride, the opinion-makers' favorite, and then a bravura capturing of the coveted audience award at Toronto.

Given this ever-expanding universe of choice, how were the dozen or so festivals profiled in this collection selected? Some, like Cannes and Sundance, were obvious choices: besides the fact that I've been going to them for a decade and more, you can't hope to understand why and how festivals function without considering the ins and outs of the biggest, brashest, and most influential of the bunch.

The other festivals investigated were not random selections. The ones I've focused on not only show films, but they also serve as picture windows onto a wider, more diverse world and cinema's place in it. Sometimes, as with Sarajevo and Havana, film is a vehicle for trying to understand the international political community's most vexing dilemmas. Sometimes, as with Burkina Faso's FESPACO and Pordenone's Giornate del Cinema Muto, it's a chance to examine the very nature of the cinematic experience. For different reasons and at different times, each of these festivals has made me feel the sense of excitement that lit up Luchino Visconti's face all those many years ago.

PART ONE

Festivals with Business Agendas

Cannes

What is this thing called Cannes?

Grueling, crowded, complicated, unforgiving, it's been likened by a survivor to "a fight in a brothel during a fire." A place where reputations are made and hearts are broken, fascinating and frustrating in equal parts, it has a love-hate relationship with Hollywood, yet gives out awards, including the Palme d'Or for best picture, that are the movie world's most coveted next to the Oscars. It's where Clint Eastwood might find himself watching — and enjoying — an Iranian film about baking bread, a place, novelist Irwin Shaw wrote, that attracted all of film: "the artists and pseudo-artists, the businessmen, the con men, the buyers and sellers, the peddlers, the whores, the pornographers, critics, hangers-on, the year's heroes, the year's failures." It's where you need a press pass to get your press pass, and where those passes come in five hierarchical (and color-coded) levels of importance. Its official name is Festival International du Film, the International Film Festival, as if there were only one, so it's no surprise that, more than anything else, Cannes is big.

Normally a city of 70,000, Cannes sees its population increase by 50 percent during the twelve days it functions as the stand-alone epicenter of the international film world. Producer David Puttnam calls it "one-stop shopping," the place where business and creative types and the people who write about them congregate. "I'm quite enjoying it," Booker Prize–winning novelist A. S. Byatt told me on her first visit in 1995. "I'm a workaholic, and everyone here is too. It's a city full of them, frantically busy. Like the ant heap."

In a kind of self-fulfilling prophecy, then, everyone is here from everywhere because everyone else is here as well, and where else are you going to run into all those people? The French pornography industry schedules its annual Hot d'Or awards to coincide with the festival, and a group of more than a hundred French railway workers/cinema enthusiasts show up annually to award the wonderfully named Rail d'Or to a deserving film. To take advantage of all this, the festival has become the world's largest yearly media event, a round-the-clock cinematic billboard that in 1999 attracted 3,893 journalists, 221 TV crews, and 118 radio stations representing 81 countries all told. And then there are the films. Don't ask about the films.

For unlike most festivals, Cannes has a film market officially attached, where international buyers swoop in to view and possibly purchase the rights to something like six hundred films displayed in thousands of screenings in nearly thirty rooms. When you add in the nearly hundred films shown at the festival proper (which is actually more like three separate festivals competing against each other), what results is a cinematic triathlon so strenuous it even exhausts the man who put it together for twenty-three years, Gilles Jacob. When the festival is over, Jacob told me once, "I go home to Paris, and I talk to no one. Not my wife, not my children. No one."

But even saying all this doesn't truly capture Cannes, an experience *Variety*'s Timothy M. Gray once characterized as not only impossible to describe to someone who's never been there but also "nearly impossible to describe to someone who has been there." Because the halls of the headquarters Palais du Festival and the streets and beaches surrounding it are a circus with an infinite number of rings, anywhere you turn reveals something you can't quite believe you're seeing.

On a day chosen at random near the end of the 2000 festival, several large TVs in the Palais were broadcasting Brian De Palma's press conference, where the *Mission to Mars* director was seen lashing out at a questioner who had the temerity to ask about aspects of "*hommage*" in his work. "It's that word again," De Palma raged, literally pointing an accusatory finger at the unsuspecting miscreant. "It's been attached to me for forty years, and no one's been able to define it. What does it mean?"

Escaping De Palma and the Palais, you nearly get run over by a roller-skating young woman simultaneously turning in circles and selling newspapers: "*Nice-Matin, Nice-Matin*," she yells as the wheels grind. Turning away, you find your hand taken by a person in a giant Mickey Mouse costume who then pulls you within camera range of a man with a Polaroid who wants to be paid for the compromising photo of you and the Mouse he's about to take. Out of the corner of your eye you see a black-robed character, his face masked and hooded, nonchalantly walk by wearing a sandwich board advertising *Demonium*, a film few people have heard of and less care about.

You try and move away, but two women from something called Pop.com, a Web site whose ultimate purpose is as darkly mysterious as *Demonium*, hand you a red balloon and a lollipop. On the beach, a crowd is forming, silently watching as a kneeling young woman gets a tattoo etched onto her shoulder. Pause for a moment to watch and two people brush past, loaded down like Sherpas with dozens of heavy plastic sacks on their shoulders. Each sack turns out to be a press kit for a film called *Dead Babies*, including, for those who've always wanted one, a *Dead Babies* travel toothbrush.

With scenes like this all around, is it any wonder that the appearance of "bad boy Dennis Rodman" to promote a film called *Cutaway* at a party featuring "a laser show, go-go cages, ribaldry, revelry and European and U.S. DJs" causes hardly a ripple?

For many film people, a first trip to Cannes is kind of a grail, a culmination that tells you, whether you're a journalist with a computer or a filmmaker walking up the celebrated red carpet to the Palais du Festival for an evening-dress only screening, that you've arrived. For me, para-doxically, it was a beginning, the first dizzying, tantalizing glimpse of a chaotic world I wanted to be part of but wasn't sure had room for me.

Cannes was celebrating its twenty-fifth festival when I first covered it in 1971 as a not-much-older reporter for the *Washington Post*. Though the event had strayed from its stated goal of being "a festival of cine-matographic art, from which all extracinematic preoccupations would be excluded," it was even then a terribly exciting place to be.

Hardly any Americans made the trip in those days, and I was rewarded with a room in a smart hotel called the Gonnet located on the Boulevard de la Croisette, the city's trademark oceanfront promenade, filled even then with crowds and crowd-pleasing eccentrics, like the elderly gentleman who pounded a cowbell and exclaimed in French, "Always the same films, always the same circus. Pollution, mental and physical pollution. Nothing, nothing, nothing."

The old festival Palais was a classic white building, small but elegant, and patrolled by a vigilant cadre of tuxedoed guards determined to evict gate crashers. I got my first taste of how surreal Cannes can be as I watched a well-dressed French interloper being almost choked to death as he was literally dragged out of the Palais by a pair of tuxedos. Yet he didn't lack the presence of mind to insist, as loudly as that chokehold would allow, "Un peu de politesse, s'il vous plait" — a bit of politeness, if you don't mind.

Because U.S. reporters, even young ones, were a rare commodity, set-ting up interviews was easy and casual. I spent a rainy afternoon with Jack Nicholson, listening to him defend his directorial debut, *Drive, He Said*, which had been screened the night before to a wave of boos. And I talked to the great Italian director Luchino Visconti, who chuckled as he told me that his visa for an upcoming American visit didn't allow him to leave New York.

"I don't know why they think I'm dangerous — maybe they think I want to kill Nixon," he said puckishly. "I have no intention of doing any subversive actions. I don't want to kill Nixon, or even Mrs. Nixon. I just want to see the rest of the country. Write this in Washington; perhaps the president will read it." I did; he didn't.

I didn't get back to Cannes until 1976, and the crowds had not abated. It was at a late-night debut of Nagisa Oshima's *In the Realm of the Senses*, whose lurid story of mutual sexual obsession leading to castration had created a ferocious want-to-see, that I got the closest I've ever been to being crushed against a wall by a surging, expectant overflow crowd. Even Oshima's images seemed tame after that.

That was also the year *Taxi Driver* won the Palme d'Or, and I watched, as surprised as he was, as youthful director Martin Scorcese got his first taste of how disconcertingly political European film journalism can be. Midway through the *Taxi Driver* press conference, a French journalist rose and referred to a scene between Robert De Niro's Travis Bickle and Jodie Foster's Iris where Travis talks about getting away from the city and spending some quiet time in the country.

"Mr. Scorcese," the journalist asked, "should we interpret that scene as Travis turning his back on bankrupt Western industrial capitalism and insisting on a more communal, socialist model for life in the future?" Scorcese looked truly, deeply baffled. "No," he said finally. "Travis just wants to spend some time in the country."

That festival also gave me an insight into the thought patterns of actors, even actors turned director. Roman Polanski was in attendance with *The Tenant*, adapted from a novel by Roland Topor, which tells the story of a man who takes over an apartment just vacated by a woman who has committed suicide and begins to feel his neighbors want him to end his life as well. Polanski played the lead in addition to directing, spending what felt like half the movie attempting suicide in drag by jumping out of an upper-story window, not succeeding, and then crawling back up the stairs, still in drag, to leap out all over again. And again.

"Mr. Polanski," I blurted out with what now seems like startling naïveté. "Why did you ever choose this film?" He looked at me with genuine surprise. "It's a great role for me, don't you think?" was his reply, and he meant it.

A bemused man with a rasping, infectious laugh that went along with an obvious streak of darkness, Polanski took advantage of the interview to tell a series of jokes to a receptive audience. My favorite concerned a man who came to a rabbi and asked, Polanski doing a fine Jewish accent, "Rabbi, I must know, am I going to heaven or hell?"

"The rabbi says, 'You come here on a Saturday to bother me about things like this?' But the man persists. 'It's become an obsession with me, rabbi. I haven't slept for three months; my wife wants to leave me; I must know.' 'All right,' says the rabbi. 'Come back next Saturday.'

"When the man comes back, the rabbi says, 'I prayed, I concentrated, I spoke with God, and I have an answer. First the good news. You're going to heaven; there's absolutely no doubt. Now the bad news. You're leaving Wednesday.'"

Don't misunderstand. It's not like this used to be some quiet little fishing village that regrettably got overrun by the glamoroids of the international film community. For more than 150 years, ever since Lord Brougham, a Lord Chancellor of England, was prevented by an outbreak of cholera from wintering in Nice in 1834 and spent his time here instead, Cannes has been a playground for the moneyed classes, home to regal hotels, chic restaurants, and pricey boutiques. Not for nothing is its sister city Beverly Hills.

And despite the French passion for cinema, there might never have been a festival here if it wasn't for the way the Italians under Mussolini and the Fascists ran the Venice Film Festival, founded in 1932. In 1937, Jean Renoir's *La Grande Illusion* was denied the top prize because of its pacifist sentiments, and the French decided if you wanted something done right you had to do it yourself.

The initial Cannes film festival (the city won out as the site after an intramural tussle with Biarritz on the Atlantic coast) was scheduled for the first three weeks of September 1939. Hollywood responded by sending over *The Wizard of Oz* and *Only Angels Have Wings* along with a "steamship of stars" including Mae West, Gary Cooper, Norma Shearer, and George Raft. The Germans, however, chose September 1, 1939 to invade Poland, and after the opening night screening of *The Hunchback of Notre Dame*, the festival was canceled and didn't start up again until 1946.

According to the genial and informative *Hollywood on the Riviera: The Inside Story of the Cannes Film Festival* by Cari Beauchamp and Henri Behar, the ambiance of that first festival was not much different from today's. They quote an excerpt from a French newspaper about the 1946 event that could have been written last year: "Here the streets are so jammed that one would think one is still in Paris. The shops are full of stuff at astronomical prices and . . . on the Croisette it is a constant parade of cars. It's the rendezvous of stars and celebrities, a whole world, half naked and tanned to a perfect crisp."

Despite its advantages, Cannes started slowly, skipping 1948 and 1950 and only getting onto an annual basis in 1951. It was in 1954 that French starlet Simone Sylva dropped her bikini top and tried to embrace Robert Mitchum in front of a horde of photographers, resulting in the kind of international press coverage that secured the festival's reputation. It had no trouble holding the world's attention, one disapproving film historian writes, because it "early opted for glamour and sensationalism" by concentrating on "the erotic fantasies of naked flesh so readily associated with a Mediterranean seaside resort."

The rival sidebar event known as the International Critics Week was begun by influential French critic Georges Sadoul in 1962, but major change didn't come to Cannes until the pivotal year of 1968. In the face of a country in turmoil, with widespread antigovernment demonstrations and upward of 10 million people in the process of going out on strike, French directors like François Truffaut and Jean-Luc Godard pushed for and achieved the cancellation of Cannes at its midway point.

A tangible result of this upheaval was the founding in the following year of another independent sidebar event, the Quinzaine des Realisateurs, or Directors' Fortnight, which continues to compete with the official festival for films and has consistently shown edgier fare ranging from Spike Lee's *She's Gotta Have It* to Todd Solondz's *Happiness*. The Quinzaine became such a threat to the festival that one of the first things Gilles Jacob did when he took over in 1978 was to start his own edgier, noncompetitive sidebar event called "Un Certain Regard."

By the time I returned to Cannes in 1992, even more had changed. The Gonnet, my first hotel, had been converted to luxury apartments, the old Palais had been torn down and replaced by the aggressively modern Noga Hilton, and a massive new Palais had replaced the chic casino next to the city's old port. Opened in 1983 at a cost of $60 million, the five-story Palais offers state-of-the-art projection in its two main theaters, the 2,400-seat Lumière and the 1,000-seat Debussy, and has so many hidden stairways, passages, and elevators I was still discovering new ones in the year 2000.

More and more, the festival had become a city within a city, taking over Cannes completely for the duration of the event. Flowers get planted two months before opening day so they'll look their best during the festival. Huge billboards on the Croisette display posters for films that are in the event as well as those that aren't but will be released later that year. A Planet Hollywood places the plaster handprints of Bruce Willis, Mel Gibson, and other stars next to a preexisting monument to Charles de Gaulle. The front of the august Carlton Hotel, a pricey survivor of the Belle Epoque, gets a different commercial makeover every year: once it featured a towering Godzilla, once a regrettably bigger than life Beavis and Butthead complete with the sentence "Huh-Huh, You Said Oui Oui," once a working Egyptian temple, including bandage-wrapped figures and life-size statues of the gods, to promote *The Mummy*. No wonder a French magazine headlined one year "Trop de Promo Tue le Cinéma," too much publicity is killing cinema.

Everywhere as well are the excesses only money and stardom can generate. Celebrity hotel guests, the *New York Times* reported, have been known to "require 150 hangers for their wardrobes and gallons of mineral water for their baths." The legendary Hôtel du Cap at Cap d'Antibes, where the German general staff luxuriated during the French occupation and where I watched Burt Lancaster dive off the rocks for an ocean swim in 1971, insists that its superpricey rooms be paid for in cash in advance.

For people tired of living in hotels, vessels like a luxury barge ("be in the middle of the business, be far from the noise" for $8,500 per day for a royal suite) or the Octopussy ("world famous, 143 foot luxury mega-yacht" costing $15,000 per day or $80,000 per week) are available. And if a regular taxi from the Nice airport is just too pokey, there are helicopters and chauffeur-driven red BMW 1100 motorcycles to be rented as well.

For those looking for a way to combine ostentation with good works, the social event of the season is always the $1,000-a-plate Cinema Against AIDS AmFAR benefit at the nearby Moulin de Mougins restaurant. In 1995, benefit chairperson Sharon Stone started the evening with a personal and emotional appeal for more funds for research and ended it by snappily auctioning off model Naomi Campbell's navel ring for $20,000 to a Saudi Arabian prince. As the bizarre bidding went back and forth, a classic Hollywood type with more money than sense wondered aloud if Stone would throw in a pair of her panties. "Anyone who has $7.50," the actress replied in a bravura Cannes moment, "knows I don't wear any."

It was at a quiet breakfast on the pristine terrace of the Hôtel du Cap that Tim Robbins, exhausted after enduring a wild all-night party that had people screaming in the hallway outside his room, succinctly encapsulated the relentless duality that is finally the trademark of this unwieldy, difficult-to-categorize festival.

"Cannes is a very strange mixture of the art of film and total prostitution of film," he said. "One of the things I remember from my first year here in 1992 is walking into a room and meeting a great actor like Gérard Depardieu and then walking out and seeing this poster of a woman with large breasts holding a machine gun. The film wasn't made yet, but they already had a title and an ad concept."

This ability to somehow combine the yin and yang of the film business, to link at the same site the rarefied elite of the world's movie artists and a brazen international marketplace where money is the only language spoken and sex and violence the most convertible currencies, is the logic-defying triumph of Cannes.

This is a festival where popcorn movies like the Sharon Stone–starring *Quick and the Dead* and *Torrente, the Dumb Arm of the Law* (advertised in its country of origin with the line "Just When You Thought Spanish Cinema Was Getting Better") share space with the work of demanding directors like Theo Angelopolous, Hou Hsiao-Hsien, and Abbas Kiarostami. Where festival head Jacob speaks with pride of attracting Madonna as well as cult director Manoel de Oliveira. Where within twenty-four hours in 1997 you could have a serious talk about the situation in Sarajevo with "Welcome to Sarajevo" director Michael Winterbottom and share a press lunch with Sylvester Stallone, who displayed an easy manner and surprising charm as he mordantly dissected past fiascoes like *Stop or My Mother Will Shoot*: "If it was a question of having my spleen removed with a tractor or watching it again, I'd say, 'Start up the engine.'"

Stallone also ridiculed the current crop of action films ("If you took the explosions out, 90 percent of them would not have endings; if someone stole the gasoline truck, it would be like an e.e. cummings poem at the end") and talked of looking forward to the gathering of all the previous Palme d'Or winners that was scheduled for later that week. "I'm gonna meet those people who won't work with me," he said, amused. "All in one room."

This uneasy but animated coexistence between the commercial and the artistic sometimes gets highlighted in a way no screenwriter could have concocted. Opening night of the 2000 festival, for instance, started with a casual screening of Ken Loach's *Bread and Roses*, an earnest film dealing with the urgent problems of labor organizers attempting to unionize impoverished, often illegal workers who make marginal livings cleaning the office towers of Los Angeles.

When that socially conscious picture was over, I hurried back to my room in the aptly named Hotel Splendid and changed from a T-shirt to a tuxedo to attend the official opening night party for *Vatel*, a big-budget French film set amid the "it's good to be the king" splendor of the profligate seventeenth-century court of the Roi du Soleil himself, Louis XIV.

Once *Vatel*'s story of a celebrated chef and master of revels, played by Gérard Depardieu, had ended, the audience walked out the door of the Lumière theater and directly into the most elaborate, extravagant, and undoubtedly expensive re-creation of the film's world. The entire entrance hall of the Palais had been changed, via billowing red curtains, huge paintings, multiple candles, and artfully faked stone walls, into a vintage French chateau. And that was just the setting.

I joined the disbelieving guests in evening clothes and walked slowly down corridors that had become the physical duplicates of what had just been seen on screen. Actors dressed in period costumes brought *Vatel*'s kitchens to life: bread was kneaded, fruit was dipped in glazes, ice was sculpted, salamis and cheeses and an enormous fresh fish were displayed, and, adding just the right touch, a man rushed through the crowd clutching a goose.

At the dinner itself, white-coated waiters poured champagne from a stream of magnums as actors playing the king and his intimates ate on a stage. By the time tabletop fireworks ended the evening, the janitors of Los Angeles seemed to belong to another universe.

The key element ensuring that the bracing presence of the commercial remains integral to Cannes is the market, officially known as MIF, Marché International du Film. It started in 1959, apparently with one flimsy twenty-seat room jerry-built onto the roof of the old Palais. Now, with its own brand-new building, the 70,000-square-foot Espace Riviera, it attracts approximately 6,000 participants representing some 1,500 companies from more than seventy countries. Many Cannes regulars agree with Ethan Coen, the writer-producer half of the Coen brothers team, that without the market Cannes would be "a little too snooty."

Every year, festival regulars keep a watch for market films with titles that go beyond the preposterous. Standouts include *Biker Mice from Mars, Teenage Bonnie and Klepto Clyde* ("Desperate Kids, Bonded by Passion and Crime"), *Headless Body in Topless Bar, Kraa! The Sea Monster* (touted as the successor to *Zarkorr! The Invader*), and the always popular *Attack of the Giant Moussaka*. One year saw a wave of kickboxing films from Korea with titles like *Year of the King Boxer* and *Kickboxer from Hell* while comedies about sumo wrestlers never seem to go out of style: *Sumo Do, Sumo Don't* was offered in 1992, and in the year 2000 *Secret Society* showcased the story of an overweight housewife somehow becoming a sumo standout.

Having these films not only for sale but also available for viewing can be a refreshing change of pace, like a dish of palate-cleansing sorbet after a constant diet of heavier, more ponderous fare. I felt nothing but elation after experiencing Jerzy Hoffman's three-hour-and-three-minute *With Fire and Sword*, a Polish *Gone with the Wind* that came complete with a handsome hero, a deranged villain, and a beautiful princess with gold braids that reached almost to the ground. Other diversions included frequent male choral singing, bare-chested Cossacks pounding enormous drums, and a sidekick with the strength of ten who has taken a vow of chastity until he cuts off three heads with a single sword stroke. "I've gotten two many times," he says mournfully, "but never three." Only in the market.

The market is also the place where films that are little more than a concept and a title make themselves known in the hopes of raising enough money (via preselling foreign distribution rights) to actually shoot the film. In 1976, I was part of a contingent of revelers that was ferried out to a large cruise ship, where energetic waiters encouraged everyone to take part in the Greek party tradition of breaking plates. Hundreds of pieces of crockery dutifully made the ultimate sacrifice to help create interest in what turned out to be *The Greek Tycoon*.

Even as the market has grown more sophisticated, that kind of bombastic showmanship has not gone away. At the 2000 festival, the talk cen-

tered on a new film from resurgent mogul Menahem Golan ("the producer and director of *Delta Force*, $100 million in world box office"), who
flooded the city with posters, flyers, and much-sought-after T-shirts for
Elian, the Gonzales-boy Story, a.k.a. "the explosive, dramatic and human
story that captured the world." Illustrated with an obviously faked photo
re-creation of Elian's celebrated rescue at gunpoint, the film swore that
it was "shooting now in a secret location." Everyone considered themselves warned.

This shameless carnival atmosphere is not for everyone, and it can be
especially tiring for stars and directors who are dragooned into promoting new films. Frenetically shuttled from one-on-ones with key journalists to group situations to TV setups to still photo opportunities, prime
interview targets can feel like valuable private railway cars being switched
from track to track as they meet literally hundreds of media representa-
tives. It's no wonder that by the time Chinese star Gong Li got to a group
press lunch in 1993 to promote *Farewell My Concubine*, she was so hungry
she ate all the rolls off the table and asked her interpreter if she could have
some of her lunch as well.

Filmmakers also don't necessarily enjoy Cannes, because, unlike
famously supportive festivals like Toronto and Telluride, it can be an
unforgiving, high-risk, hostile place. Boos not infrequently clash with
cheers after competition screenings, so much so that even as much of a
Cannes partisan as head man Gilles Jacob has admitted "the commenta-
tors are merciless. There are festivals where you can send a film thinking that if it doesn't go down well, it may do OK in the long run. That's
not possible at Cannes. Cannes is very violently for or against."

One form of dismay that is unique to Cannes is an activity I've come
to call "thumping." The seats in the Palais snap back with a resounding
sound when their occupants get up to leave, so when disgruntled viewers exit a screening before a film is finished, everyone knows about it.
"There is something terrifying in the new Palais," is how a publicist
quoted in their book described one unfortunate screening to authors

Beauchamp and Behar. "People were so bored they started leaving after an hour in droves. In packs. It went *clack clackclackclack clackclack clack*. You felt repeatedly stabbed in the back. Each clack was terrifying. And it's still terrifying. Those clacks remain engraved."

But no matter what they think about the dark and chaotic sides of the Cannes experience, even the unlikeliest filmmakers in the end are almost compelled to attend because it is so big, because so much worldwide publicity can be generated from here.

John Sayles and his producing partner Maggie Rienzi, called in one profile people who "will never be mistaken for the sort of couple who attract the paparazzi in Cannes," show up and, yes, attract photographers. "Being here is a job," explained Todd Solondz, who arrived with his genially twisted *Happiness*. "The picture doesn't sell itself, I have to sell it, especially since I don't exactly have a 'big opening weekend' kind of cast." Even Ken Loach, the dean of socially conscious British filmmakers, dons formal wear for the red-carpet premiers of his films. "There are bigger things to be rebellious about," Loach reminded me, "than black tie."

So it turns out, as with any big, glamorous party, that the people who are most upset about Cannes are those who can't get in. In recent years that has meant filmmakers from both Germany and Italy, two major film-producing nations that have had enormous trouble getting their pictures accepted into the official competition, the most prestigious part of Cannes.

The 2000 festival was the seventh year in a row that German filmmakers were shut out of the competition, and they were not happy about it. "We suffer when this happens," one German director told the *Hollywood Reporter*, which detailed that "since 1994, both Taiwan and China/Hong Kong have had four films each in competition; Denmark has had three; Iran, Greece and Japan have each had two; and Mexico, Belgium and Mali have each had one. During that time, Germany, which has the world's second-largest media industry and which has a newly booming feature film sector, has had none." The reason for the snub, another director theorized, was the French belief that "France invented culture, and the Germans can't possibly participate."

Even more unhappy, and not at all unwilling to talk about it, were the Italians when they, too, were shut out of Cannes 2000. Veteran producer Dino DeLaurentiis was quoted as saying "These snotty Frenchmen make me laugh. In an international festival, it's ridiculous to exclude our cinema." Film director Ricky Tognazzi, retribution on his mind, said "For a year I will avoid eating French goat cheese." Christian De Sica, son of the great director Vittorio De Sica, added the coup de grace: "As if the French didn't also make a lot of stupid movies."

If there is one thing that is generally agreed about the official competition, it's that the selection process is baffling at best. Every Cannes veteran has his or her list of ridiculous films that were somehow let in, from the dim British comedy *Splitting Heirs* to the literally unreleasable Johnny Depp-directed *The Brave* to the even worse Steven Soderbergh *Schizopolis* (shown as an out-of-competition special event).

Even worse, if films with any kind of crowd-pleasing potential do get into the festival, they are often relegated to meaningless out-of-competition slots. Such was the fate of deservedly popular works like *Strictly Ballroom, Priscilla, Queen of the Desert, Trainspotting,* and *Crouching Tiger, Hidden Dragon.* This trend is so well known that comedy writer-director Francis Veber, the most widely popular French filmmaker of his generation (*The Tall Blond Man with One Black Shoe, La Chèvre, Les Compères*) genially told me that when he received a phone call from the festival announcing an official tribute to him in 1999, "I was so surprised I fell on my ass. Why the tribute now? Maybe they've seen my tests for cholesterol and sugar, and they think I will die soon."

The uncomfortable truth is that for a film festival that is the cynosure of all eyes, Cannes's taste, at least as far as the competition goes, is surprisingly narrow. France is the home of the auteur theory, which deifies directors at the expense of other creative parties, and Cannes overwhelmingly favors films by critically respectable auteurs who've been there before, a usual-suspects group of largely noncommercial filmmakers *Variety* categorizes as "heavyweight helmers." It's proved to be an increasingly unpopular philosophy.

"High Art pays low dividends at Cannes fest" was the headline on a much-talked-about 1999 piece by chief *Variety* film critic Todd McCarthy that placed the auteur theory in "an advanced state of decrepitude" and lamented that "the gulf between the sort of High Art films that many serious directors want to make (and that is generally sought by fests) and pictures that will hold some sort of interest for audiences is bigger than ever."

In the same vein, Maurice Huleu of *Nice-Matin* wondered if "this outpouring of work, of talent and creativity is predestined to satisfy only a few initiates." Talking of the 1997 decision, which split the Palme d'Or between rarefied films by Iran's Abbas Kiarostami and Japan's Shohei Immamura, Huleu emphasized that the jury "may have sacrificed other considerations in the name of art, but they also did a disservice to the Cannes Festival and to cinema."

Which brings us, inevitably, to Hollywood, that other center of the movie universe. It's the place that makes the movies the world hungers for, and though Cannes well knows the value of glamour and glitz, the festival in recent years has had great difficulty attracting top-drawer items from the bowels of the studio system. So Cannes 2000, for instance, settled for Brian De Palma's frigid *Mission to Mars* while even the most aesthetically rigorous French journalists and critics were wondering why *Gladiator* wasn't there in its stead.

There are reasons for this absence. Cannes, unlike Toronto, comes in the spring, the wrong time of year for the "quality" films studios would prefer to send to festivals. Cannes, as noted, can kill your picture, something studios don't want to risk with prospective blockbusters costing tens of millions of dollars. Cannes is expensive, especially when you factor in flying stars over in private jets. And, especially in recent years, the festival hierarchy has been unwilling to play the Hollywood game, to take trips to Los Angeles and do the kind of schmoozing and flattering of the powers that be that's necessary to overturn more rational considerations.

Also a factor is that the jury awards at Cannes can be so arbitrary and contrived, so governed by whim and geared toward advancing political and cultural agendas, that studio pictures rarely get what Hollywood considers a fair shake. For every year like 1993, when the Palme d'Or was wisely split between *The Piano* and *Farewell My Concubine*, there is a 1999, when the David Cronenberg–led jury horrified everyone except themselves by giving three major awards to the unwatchable *L'Humanité*. "David Cronenberg's decisions," one festival veteran said, "are scarier than his films." In 1992, the brilliant French-Canadian *Leolo* was shut out at least in part because its director, Jean-Claude Lauzon, made a provocative sexual remark to an American actress who was on the jury. "When I said it," the director recalled, "my producer was next to me and he turned gray." In an atmosphere like this, it's no wonder one of the best Hollywood films of the past decade, *L.A. Confidential*, made it into the competition and came home with nothing. Not exactly the kind of encouragment the studios are looking for.

Yet when a film hits here, when it wins a major award and touches a nerve in the audience, it really hits. Quentin Tarantino was genuinely shocked when his *Pulp Fiction* took the Palme in 1994 ("I don't make the kinds of movies that bring people together, I make the kinds of movies that split people apart"), but that moment was the engine of the film's enormous worldwide success. Steven Soderbergh had already won a prize at Sundance, but when he became the youngest person to win a Palme for *sex, lies and videotape*, he said the experience was "like being a Beatle for a week. It was so unexpected, like someone saying 'You've just won $10 million' and sticking a microphone in your face. I didn't know how to react, I don't know what I said." And then there was Roberto Benigni.

Benigni's *Life Is Beautiful* didn't win the Palme in 1998 (that went to Theo Angelopoulos's understandably forgotten *Eternity and a Day*); it took the runner-up Grand Prize, but it mattered not. A direct line could probably be traced from Benigni's effusive behavior that night, running on stage and passionately kissing jury president Martin Scorcese's feet, to its eventual status as a triple Oscar winner and the then highest-grossing foreign-language film in U.S. history. That indelible image of Benigni in ecstasy will likely do as much for the status and mythology of Cannes as the earlier shot of Simone Sylva going topless with Robert Mitchum did for this festival of festivals so many years ago.

Sundance

He materialized all at once in a crowded room, his eyes wide and next door to desperate, his grip on my shoulder firm, even insistent. "See my film," he said, quiet but intense. "Change my life."

At any other film event in any other city, that moment with a young director might have seemed unreal, out of place, even threatening. But this was the Sundance Film Festival in Park City, Utah, the flagship of the burgeoning American independent film movement and a dream factory for the modern age, where, as Warner Baxter said to Ruby Keeler in *42nd Street*, "You're going out a youngster, but you've got to come back a star."

It happened to Kevin Smith after his *Clerks* debuted here in 1994: "When I came to Sundance, I was a wage slave. And then, twenty-four hours later, I had a filmmaking career." It happened to Ed Burns, now known as one of the stars of *Saving Private Ryan* and a director in his own right but then working as a grunt at "Entertainment Tonight" until *The Brothers McMullen* screened at Sundance: "Nothing has been the same since. The lights went down, the movie starts and the audience starts laughing. And then afterwards, agents, production companies, and distribution companies — right then and there — the bidding war begins."

It happened to Steven Soderbergh, whose unheralded *sex, lies and*

31

videotape took the audience award and went on to win the Palme d'Or at Cannes, gross $24 million, and create a directing career that blossomed with the Julia Roberts–starring *Erin Brockovich*. It happened on a bigger scale to the modest *Blair Witch Project*, which cost $100,000, sold for just over $1 million after a midnight screening, and ended up grossing $140 million and putting its formerly scruffy trio of filmmakers onto the covers of *Time* and *Newsweek* and into the carefully groomed center of a high-gloss ad for Dewar's scotch. Such is the power of Sundance.

That one particular festival held every January in a ski town thirty-something miles from Salt Lake City—a tourist-dependent hamlet "somehow both pristine and fake" (in critic David Denby's words) that likes to boast about having five hundred realtors and more chefs per capita than Paris, France—should have this kind of a transformative gift has been lost on absolutely no one.

While 250 films applied for the festival's dramatic competition in 1995, that number had more than tripled, to 849 films looking for but sixteen places, by the year 2000. Documentary entrants shot up from 220 in 1999 to 347 in 2000, a jump of 57 percent for the same sixteen spaces in just twelve months. The twenty-nine slots in World Cinema attracted 450 hopeful films, with directors who got in happy to make the trek from as far away as Bhutan and Tajikistan, two of the remoter parts of Asia. Perhaps most impressive was that but sixty short films were chosen from an almost terrifying 1,928 applicants.

"I meet people in so many walks of life and they're always grabbing a camera," says festival director Geoffrey Gilmore, both heartened and unnerved by that torrent of cinema. "People used to go to a garret and paint. Now it's 'I'm a filmmaker.'" Adds Steven Soderbergh, who ought to know, "making a movie has sort of crept up on being a rock star on the fantasy list for most people."

For a town with a population in the area of 6,000, the growth in attendance—it's now estimated that more than 20,000 show up annually—has been equally unnerving. The festival expanded from 15,750 seats sold in 1985 to 135,922 in 1999, an increase of almost 900 percent.

And that doesn't count the great numbers of people who take advantage of the area's ever-increasing supply of condominiums built for skiers to show up without tickets on the increasingly unlikely chance they will stumble onto some.

At the 2000 festival, for instance, people stood on the waiting list line for the world premier of *American Psycho* for four hours without getting in (they can count themselves lucky), and other ticketless individuals have been known to show up with sleeping bags at the festival's outdoor box office as early as a frigid 3:50 A.M. to wait for released tickets. As the crowds increase, it's closer to truth than hyperbole when master documentarian Errol Morris (*Fast, Cheap and Out of Control, The Thin Blue Line*) waspishly says he prepares for trips to the festival by "spending seventy-two hours in a meat locker with people I don't like, and all of them have cell phones."

If further proof is wanted of this festival's preeminence and influence, it can be found in the ever-growing number of competing/complementary events that take place in Park City at the same time as Sundance, attempting with some success to latch onto whatever individuals can't procure tickets and won't be bothered with standing on those interminable lines.

Very much first among equals among the alternatives is Slamdance, founded as a salon de refusés by four directors whose films were turned down by Sundance and who initially grandly called their event "Slamdance '95, Anarchy in Utah: The First Annual Guerrilla International Film Festival." Helped by the scorn of Sundance Institute president Robert Redford, who grumbled about "a festival that's attached itself to us in a parasitical way," Slamdance has grown into something of a venerable institution itself, with over 2,000 films applying for slots and road show versions traveling to New York, Los Angeles, Washington D.C., London, and even Cannes. Not bad for a fest that was, to quote Redford again, "born out of rejection."

Aside from Slamdance, some of the more prominent rivals include No Dance, "acclaimed as the world's first and only DVD-projected film festival," and Slamdunk, which made a name for itself showing Nick Broomfield's *Kurt and Courtney* documentary amid the mounted heads at the local Elks Hall after Sundance canceled its screening due to threats of legal action. More amorphous but very much present are such entities as Lapdance, DigiDance, Dances with Films, and Son of Sam Dance, which turned out to be a Toyota van with a projector attached to its roof. Even author Ken Kesey got into the act, claiming tongue-in-cheek that he was "going to organize the Slim Chance Festival. You will have to have received a number of rejections to qualify."

Though it lasted only one year, Slumdance is one of the more fondly remembered alternatives. Set up in a 6,000-square-foot basement that was once a Mrs. Fields cookie factory, Slumdance was started by a hang-loose group who called themselves Slumdance Programming Vagrants and managed 150 submissions before opening night. As their press release headline nicely put it, "Slumdance Stuns Movie World by Existing."

The Slumdance gang literally outfitted their basement like a mock slum. You entered through a mission area that served free soup, past a Tent City (individual video areas designed like hobo housing) and entered the Lounge, the main screening area outfitted with projectors, couches, and sleeping bags. Around the corner and behind a curtain was a set of concrete steps leading nowhere in particular. Not surprisingly, it was dubbed the Stairway to Acquisitions.

Equally inventive were the mock festivals dreamed up by the local alternative newspaper, the *Park City Ear*. One year it was Sleazedance, "a combination of exhibitionism and porn," which planned to show features like *Jeremiah's Johnson* in "a lime-green Volkswagen Vanagon with tassels on the headlights." This gave way to Skindance, the name changed for "credibility," which highlighted *Anna Lands the King, Adult Toy Story 2*, and *The Talented Mr. Strip-Me*. With Sundance showing films like *American Pimp* and *Sex: The Annabel Chong Story*, there were days when you couldn't tell Skindance from the real thing.

What all this means is that Sundance has become more than just the mother ship for the American independent movement, more than the premier showcase for films that don't march to Hollywood's drum. Because the festival and the independent scene grew up together, because they nurtured each other and made each other strong, Sundance has become America's preeminent film event and, says Lory Smith in his *Party in a Box* history of Sundance, "arguably one of the most influential film festivals in the world." This is a highly unlikely situation for a part of the world where ten feet of snow can accumulate in ten days and a town that had hardly any movie theaters and none within walking distance of each other. Though careful planning has allowed the festival to pretty much keep pace with its growing importance, it was happenstance more than anything else that put it in Park City in the first place.

If anything made this town a good match for the festival, it's a rambunctious history as what "Walking through Historic Park City" calls "one of the largest bonanza camps in the West," the source of enough silver, lead, and zinc to create the fortune of William Randolph Hearst's millionaire father George. At its zenith Park City boasted sixteen houses in its Red Light District as well as twenty-seven saloons, one of which was robbed by George "Butch Cassidy" Parker. And from 1926 on, it had its own movie theater, the Egyptian, apparently a replica of Warner's Egyptian in Pasadena and, to quote "Walking through" again, "one of only two Egyptian revival–style buildings in Utah."

Though I experienced a lot of Sundance history, I wasn't there at the beginning. As detailed in Smith's book, the festival started in 1978 in Salt Lake City and, though immediately interested in films made regionally outside the studio system, it had to go through several incarnations and numerous name changes — from the U.S. Film Festival to the Utah/U.S. Film Festival to the United States Film & Video Festival to the Sundance/United States Film Festival to Sundance — to get to where it is today.

It was director Sydney Pollack, or so the story goes, who suggested to the powers that be in 1980 that "you ought to move the festival to Park City and set it in the wintertime. You'd be the only film festival in the world held in a ski resort during ski season, and Hollywood would beat down the door to attend."

Involved in the festival, almost from the beginning, was local resident Robert Redford, who had purchased land in the Wasatch Mountains as far back as 1969. Redford, related by marriage to Sterling Van Wagenen, the festival's first director, was chairman of its board of directors and the key figure in eventually having his cultural-minded, multidisciplinary arts organization, the Sundance Institute, take on the festival in 1985 and eventually change the name in 1991. Lory Smith, one of the festival's founders, claims in his book, "We were on the cusp of success whether Sundance had become involved or not," adding "Sundance seemed determined from the outset to rewrite the festival's history as well as its own — to make it seem as if they had rescued a small-time festival from obscurity." Still, it's undeniable, as Smith himself reports, that Sundance's involvement "catapulted the festival into the stratosphere of press and public attention," which is where I found it.

My first festival visit was in 1986, when I didn't know enough to bring a heavy coat, skiers still looked down their poles at outnumbered movie interlopers, and the state's beverage consumption laws, once almost Talmudic in complexity, had changed enough to allow the local Chamber of Commerce to boast that "Utah's newly revised liquor laws are almost normal now."

Though it had been in Park City for five years, the event itself still had some of the sleepy spirit that Errol Morris remembers from showing his pet-cemetery themed *Gates of Heaven* at the 1982 festival, only the second to be held in Park City. "There was a snowstorm, I was staying in a godforsaken condo and I only had a small idea where it was located," Morris remembers. "I had to hitchhike back there, and I was picked up by people who'd been in the theater and had hated the movie. They asked me what I thought, and since I had no alternative means of transportation, I said I, too, was extremely disappointed."

I didn't attend Sundance on a regular basis until the 1992 festival, by which time I'd acquired a reliable winter coat, and American audiences,

increasingly let down by the unadventurous, lowest-common-denomi-
nator nature of Hollywood production, were acquiring a taste for what
Sundance was providing, films that the festival itself amusingly carica-
tured in a clever, albeit self-satisfied thirty-second spot that began every
screening at the 1996 festival.

A project of an ad/film class at Pasadena's Art Center College of
Design, the spot opened on a unusual assembly line, with impassive
workers taking identical cans of film and pushing them through slots of
the same size, again and again and again.

But wait. Here's a film that doesn't fit. Alarm bells go off, a crack
emergency team appears and thrusts the oversized can into a yellow box
marked "Sundance International Film Festival." "Where do they take
it?" someone asks as the offending item disappears inside a departing
truck. A coworker gives a laconic, one-word answer: "Utah."

Almost every year of its existence, Sundance has managed to discover at
least one memorable dramatic film. Aside from the features already
mentioned, debuts included *The Waterdance, In the Soup, Four Weddings
and a Funeral* (its American premier), *The Usual Suspects, Living in
Oblivion, Big Night, Ulee's Gold, Girlfight,* and *You Can Count on Me.* And
that's only the dramatic features.

On the documentary side, things were even stronger, and Sundance
soon got a deserved reputation for being the country's top nonfiction
showcase. The momentum for *Hoop Dreams,* perhaps the best, most-
influential documentary of the past decade, began here, as it did for
Crumb, Theremin, Fast, Cheap and Out of Control, and *Unzipped.* When
the Academy of Motion Picture Arts and Sciences changed its rules for
becoming a documentary finalist in 2000, a rule partially inspired by
Hoop Dreams's previous exclusion, six of the twelve features selected had
appeared at Sundance in 1999 and a seventh was set for a Slamdance
premier.

Though the concept soon became a ruinous cliché, Sundance in fact
often was the place where you could see talent early. Here was Ashley

Judd in *Ruby in Paradise*, her first major role, easily the friendliest person in town. Here was Quentin Tarantino in a Q&A session after the premier of *Reservoir Dogs* brazenly telling a viewer upset about the violence, "I don't have to justify it, I love it." And here was Trey Parker, in Sundance with the slashingly irreverent animated short *The Spirit of Christmas*, talking about improvising the obscene dialogue with codirector Matt Stone in his basement while his mom was making fudge upstairs. And there was this little series called *South Park* in the offing as well.

Because of what it stood for, Sundance became a prime spot to hear the war stories of filmmakers who were almost literally burning to get their projects completed, who talked about overcoming their difficulties with the kind of messianic zeal that *In the Soup* director Alexandre Rockwell had in mind when he said, "It's great to meet filmmakers who are as crazy as I am and as desperate to make their films." For example:

• Todd Solondz, whose *Welcome to the Dollhouse* won the Grand Jury Prize in 1996, reminisced about his first brush with fame, when his NYU short film *Schatt's Last Shot* created a fuss. When he told his then-agent he just wanted to meet some of these new people, she started crying on the phone, and when he was cornered by a trio from another agency, "one of them got down on his knees and begged. You read about things like this but it's true, it happens."

Soon Solondz had simultaneous three-picture deals with two different studios who crazily bickered about the release order of these unmade films. "It turned out the only thing I liked about these deals was telling everyone I had them. I wasn't interested in any of the pictures that came my way, and none of my friends could sympathize: 'Poor Todd, he has these two three-picture deals.'" He ended up leaving the movie business for a job teaching English as a second language (a profession he wrote into his next feature, *Happiness*), and whenever anyone asked him about his previous life, "I said I'd been working as a computer programmer, which ended conversation right there."

- Writer-director Toni Kalem, whose *A Slipping-Down Life* portrayed a woman fixated on a rock singer, told an appropriately obsessive tale about how her film ended up in the 1999 festival. Herself an actress (she was Gianelli in *Private Benjamin* and has a part in *The Sopranos*), Kalem said she'd been interested in turning the Anne Tyler novel into a film for nearly two decades ("since I pilfered the book from Random House when I worked there as a secretary") and originally wanted to play the starring role herself.

  "Other people buy houses or buy cars, I had a 'Slipping-Down Life' habit," Kalem explained. "I took acting jobs just to pay for the option. I had horrible, horrible moments when I thought someone else would do it; I once took the red-eye to New York to save my option. Everyone said, 'Toni, you've done enough, let it go.' But I said, 'If I can't do it my way, I'll keep optioning it; I'll come up here in a walker if I have to.'"

- Marc Singer, the director of *Dark Days*, the most talked-about documentary in the 2000 festival and the winner of the audience award, the freedom of expression award, and half of the cinematography award, had a back story as strong and compelling as his on-screen material.

  More than five years in the making, *Dark Days* deals with the people who live in Manhattan's underground train tunnels. A former model, the British-born Singer not only lived underground with his subjects for two years, he used them as his entire crew. More an advocate for the homeless than a filmmaker, he conceived of *Dark Days* strictly as a way to earn money to get these people above ground and rented his first camera without even knowing how to load it. "I just wanted to get them out," he said simply. "They deserve better than that."

If Sundance had a turning point event in recent years, something that showed just how important a Park City debut could be for a project, it came in 1996. That's when the Australian *Shine*, the Scott Hicks–directed film about pianist David Helfgott, a child prodigy who descended into madness, debuted as an out-of-competition world premier. It's not only that the film's first two screenings led to frenzied standing ovations; that was not unusual for Sundance. It's that everyone recognized that, as a throwback to the best kind of Hollywood movies, able to move a mass audience without insulting it, *Shine* was almost sure to be a multi-Oscar nominee. (It in fact got seven, including best picture, and won the best actor Oscar for star Geoffrey Rush.) More than that, it was deliriously up for grabs.

"I'm too old for this," one not-very-old acquisition executive said to me in the midst of the chaos that erupted around Hicks when the second screening ended. Other executives, however, were less ambivalent. Miramax's Harvey Weinstein, who'd maneuvered his company to pre-eminence in the independent world by not letting films like *Shine* escape him, thought he had a deal with Pandora, the company handling *Shine*'s overseas sale, but it was not to be.

Against considerable odds, Mark Ordesky of Fine Line Features spearheaded what he called an "in-the-condo, in-the-room, nobody-leaves-or-the-deal-is-off" negotiation to bag the film. Weinstein was beside himself, threatening to sue to get the North American rights and loudly and publicly berating Pandora's representative in a Park City restaurant. Miramax and its parent company Disney ended up with the rights in certain key overseas territories, but Robert Redford had the last word. "We do very simple things to provide entertainment here," he said at the festival's awards show. "We leave it to the snow and to Harvey Weinstein."

The much-publicized fuss over *Shine* put a spotlight on how and why Sundance, which had changed considerably over its short life, had metamorphosized. Ever since Redford's Sundance Institute had taken over the festival, the putative specter of the evil empire of Hollywood and the movie establishment had hung over the event. Every year, agents and development executives made the trek to Park City in greater and greater numbers, paying up to $5,000 for coveted Fast Passes to the entire festival and prowling the occasionally snowy streets on a lonely mission to discover the Next New Thing. As veteran independent director Victor Nunez, a two-time winner of the Grand Jury Prize (*Gal Young 'Un* in 1979, *Ruby in Paradise* in 1993) put it, "Sundance has always been a two-edged sword. On the one hand, the recognition is wonderful. On the other, that sword has always pointed west, and festival success is the calling card to making it into the establishment world."

The more certain Sundance films broke through commercially, the more distribution companies came and bought without looking back, conveniently ignoring other Sundance films that had proved to be over-hyped and overexpensive once they got down to sea level. Executives might take annual vows of abstinence, but no one remembered over-priced box office disappointments like *House of Yes*, *Slam*, *Hurricane Streets*, *Happy, Texas*, *The Castle*, and *The Spitfire Grill* when something hot and new appeared on the horizon.

All this fuss attracted the media and those who understood how to use it. "Sundance is actually an old Indian word that means publicity; few people know that," actor Eric Stoltz tartly informed *Us* magazine, and Sony Pictures Classics codirector Tom Bernard told the *New York Times* that "Sundance has the biggest concentration of press in the country. It's better than a junket. We get interviews and stories placed on our movies we couldn't get if we weren't at Sundance."

Both Robert Redford and Harvey Weinstein are masters at handling the media. When Weinstein announces his annual party, journalists rearrange their schedules so as not to miss it. In 1995, he hosted an event at the pricey Stein Erickson Lodge at which Redford himself, in effect Sundance's uncrowned king, decided to make a rare social appearance.

As soon as Redford arrived, Weinstein, shrewd as well as gracious as a host, brought him over to a table where critics and journalists from *Newsweek*, *Variety*, the *Los Angeles Times*, and the *New York Times* were sitting. Redford nodded to everyone, and, since there were no more chairs, immediately went down on one knee to have a more intimate chat with one of the most powerful critics there. Observing this tableau was Weinstein, never without words or unwilling to use them. "So Bob," he said in a voice loud enough to make the actor blush, "that's how you get those good reviews."

Though it still believes passionately in championing striving young filmmakers, Sundance itself, not immune to all the success that surrounded it, has become established and institutionalized enough to have an annual budget of $8.5 million. With a fleet of Mercedes M-Class vans as "official vehicles" and a catalog as fat and glossy as an issue of *Architectural Digest*, Sundance increasingly exudes the prosperity and success that go with its place in the film universe.

The festival catalog is as weighty as it is in part because of advertising from the festival's 125 sponsors, carefully organized into categories called Leadership, Major, Supporting, Official, and Festival. Corporations that would do credit to a Super Bowl telecast (Mercedes-Benz, AT&T, Apple, Blockbuster) lined up with less likely suspects like the San Miguel, Agua Calienta, Pechanga, and Viejas California Indian tribes and the makers of Altoids, which gave away so many mints one year that, their intrepid publicist announced, "If all of the Altoids were dropped from a helicopter over the festival center of Park City at the same time, they would blanket the area to a depth of 2.37 inches." With a festival audience both young (57 percent are between eighteen and thirty-five) and well funded (38 percent earn over $100,000), is it any wonder that the institute has expanded operations to include the Sundance Catalogue, the Sundance Channel, and Sundance Theaters?

Though people could and did argue over whether all this was good or bad for the festival, the fact that it brought increasing numbers of visitors to town (enough, apparently, to have spent over $25 million, including lodging and transportation, during the 1999 event) was undeniable. Cell phone usage during the fest rose 550 percent over the town's normal rate, and restaurants were booked a month ahead of time, with one establishment demanding a $60 food minimum per person as the price of reserving a table.

Sundance tries hard to cope with this influx, training "crowd liaison" personnel and fine-tuning the festival's different sections, their locations, even the event's invaluable but increasingly complex shuttle bus system. And, at the most basic level, this may be the only festival that regularly adds theaters in a Sisyphean attempt to keep pace with its audience.

Starting with the venerable Egyptian, a tiny triplex called the Holiday Village, and an assembly room in a hotel, Sundance added a 500-seat theater in the town's former high school (which now houses the local library), tacked on one more in a different hotel, and spearheaded local voter approval for the Eccles Theater, named after a local philanthropist, a 1,000-seat structure (which doubles as a performing arts complex when the festival is not in session) that opened in 1998 and promptly filled up.

Though some local residents (like the high school kids who agreed to carpool during the festival and rented their parking passes for $200 each, funds going to the fine arts department) try and make the best of these massive crowds, the relationship between the town and the festival that fills its streets to overflowing with "L.A.liens" is not always ideal. As "Sundance — at a glance," a brochure subtitled "An Unofficial, Personal, Native, Local, Insider's Survival Guide to the Sundance Film Festival," notes, the alleged financial boost notwithstanding, "it's no great boon to replace ski tourists who spend thousands on vacation with people who eat off grocery salad bars."

It's the local alternative papers that turn out to be hardest on the festival. "Get Your Black Leather Out, It's Time to Be Scene," headlined the *Salt Lake City Weekly*, recycling the worn cliché that visitors are all PIBS (People In Black) who slip and slide on icy streets in their stiletto heels and/or Gucci footwear. Typical was a column in Park City's *Mountain Times* headlined "The Festival We All Love to Hate," which noted that "During Sundance week Park City virtually reeks with a desperate need to be seen as somehow relevant and important in a town overflowing with relevant and important personages. . . . This is the place where people who fancy themselves power brokers come to broker their power; this is the place where outsiders try to become insiders, and where the insiders are as plentiful as the slush in the streets."

Yet for all this carping and borderline sniveling, for all the people (invariably New Yorkers) who insist Sundance has become a twin to Los Angeles, the core feeling of the festival, its fundamental nature, has remained surprisingly unchanged albeit a bit harder to find under all the accoutrements of success.

It's a shaggy, countercultural essence, defined by the filmmakers themselves: invariably youthful, inevitably walking the streets in packs, determinedly pasting posters to every available blank space and giving the place a summer-camp-in-winter ambiance. It's a feeling one film-maker summarized by saying his work was "made entirely without adult supervision," a convivial vitality that British playwright David Hare, attending for the first time in 2000, noticed at once. "It seems a very big dating festival, with a lot of hip young people teeming with hormones, sexual spores," he said. A gray-haired attendee, whose name I never did get, put it another way when he saw me, a complete stranger, at the far end of a long hallway and immediately broke into a grin. The smile widened as we got closer and just as we were passing he whispered bemusedly in my ear, "Another old guy."

Personally I tend to love the spirit of the place: the filmmakers on the street handing out cards and hustling an audience for their work, the director I met one year wandering the halls of the Yarrow Hotel stopping strangers and asking for $8 million in completion funds. And of course those ever-present signs and posters, like one at a box office saying "Way Sold Out" and another thoughtfully advising ticket sellers to "avert misunderstanding by calm, poise, balance."

The posters for individual films, especially for shorts and fringe items desperate to attract an audience, can be cleverer than the pictures themselves. "No Stars! No Action! No Sex! In Color!" for something called *Trigger Happy* was a personal favorite in 1999, and 2000 saw a flyer for *Johnny Greyeyes* headlined "Who is crying now???" and explaining, "I have spent three years and all my money making this movie. All my friends hate me and my girlfriend left me. But you know what? It looks pretty good. Come and check it out."

One of the most memorable guerrilla campaigns was mounted in 1994 for an Estonian/Finnish coproduction called *Darkness in Tallinn*. It not only kept coming up with new wrinkles for its zany photocopied fliers ("Dare to Cast the First Estone" read one, "Starring Sly Estallone and Sharon Estone" another, "Everybody Must Get Estoned" a third); it also started its screenings with a live a cappella version of what the film's director and producer claimed to be the Estonian national anthem.

Similar events happen frequently in Sundance theaters, adding to the festival's off-center charm. When a screening of *Rhythm Thief* was delayed for technical reasons during the 1995 festival, director Matthew Harrison (who'd shot the thing in eleven days for $11,000) sang a chorus of "There's No Business Like Show Business" to keep the audience entertained. When the delay at another film reached an hour, the staff at the Egyptian theater took pity on the audience and handed out free sticks of Twizzlers red licorice. And Arthur Nakane, an L.A.-based one-man band and the subject of a short called *Secret Asian Man* showed up with all his instruments during the 2000 event and had people literally go-go dancing in the aisles of the tiny Holiday Village cinema. Believe me, this sort of thing doesn't happen at Cannes.

This kind of energy tends to be contagious. In 1994, for instance, a group of twenty-four exuberant students from a filmmaking program at Pacoima Junior High outside of Los Angeles came en masse as the festival's partial guests, supplied with free tickets by Sundance but having had to spend the entire year, in classic Judy Garland–Mickey Rooney fashion, raising money to pay their expenses.

"We sold hundreds of boxes of chocolates, blow pops, gummy bears, gummy worms, everything there is that's gummy, and if you counted each of the M&Ms we sold, it was in the millions," said student Josh Gray-Emmer. Was it worth it? "We've been at other festivals, but since we're kids, we don't always get a really good response," said fellow student Megwynn White. "But here we can go up to directors, say, 'Hi, we're students' and actually talk to them."

Also typical, in another way, was twenty-nine-year-old aspiring writer-director Garry Dinnerman, a graduate of Georgia State's film school whose short, *Outside Looking In*, was turned down by the 1996 festival.

Nothing deterred, Dinnerman rented a corner room at the Treasure Mountain Inn on Main Street, hung a banner advertising his film from the balcony, and even projected a slide announcing screenings to be held in his room on the wall of a building across the street, next to a Mrs. Fields sign. He faxed notices of his intention to about two hundred potential viewers and spent much of his time in that hotel room (which had a prankish faked autographed photo of Robert Redford calling *Outside Looking In* "truly the best short film I've ever seen" on the door) waiting for an audience to arrive.

"If I could have somebody from Fine Line or Touchstone or an agent come by and look at it, I'll be happy," he said cheerfully. Only six people showed up the first day, but Dinnerman was undaunted. "The festival," he said, "is just getting started."

Given all of this, it is hard not to be taken by the Sundance Festival, and almost everyone is. Yet it's gotten harder and harder to return every year without noticing that the event has a core flaw, something that infrequent visitors don't notice and regulars shrug off, a flaw in, of all places, the dramatic competition. This is the section that gets the most filmmaker interest and the most publicity, yet it's also the one that Sundance regulars would count as the weakest and most disappointing.

Despite, or maybe because of, the festival's success, there has been an increasing disconnect between how large and prestigious it's gotten and a stubborn insistence on focusing this most celebrated event on films that seem almost perversely picked to conform to a narrow and out-moded aesthetic agenda, films that feel as if they're making the cut because they will never reach a wider audience.

Despite the number of successful films that have debuted at Sundance, it's difficult to escape the feeling that the competition selection process has an unmistakable anticommercial bias. This may sound noble and honorable, but in reality it's a counterproductive exercise in artistic elitism that does the independent movement no good at all.

What viewers often see is a string of earnest, well-meaning films that are as sensitive and artistic in intent as anyone could want, but have zero chance of pleasing audiences outside of a festival's rarefied atmosphere — and frequently not much of one even there. While no one outside the studio system would argue that just being commercial makes a film good, it's equally true, though by no means accepted at Sundance, that just being noncommercial doesn't automatically confer worthiness either. Yes, there are wonderful films there is no large audience for, and those have a place at the festival, but just because there's no audience for a given film doesn't make it by definition wonderful.

For many years, that dynamic was typified by Sundance's steadfast patronage of painfully self-absorbed films made by and about disaffected young people trying to make sense of their alienated lives. One year, in the weeks leading up to Sundance, I joined entertainment writer Gregg Kilday in a pre-festival Los Angeles screening of such an item, a film that was such a classically morose Sundance item about sullen teenagers confused about their sexuality that when the lights went up Gregg and I looked at each other, shook our heads, and just laughed. It was such a Sundance film, Gregg said, he'd reflexively reached under his seat for his parka when the credits started to roll.

This anticommercial bias has infected Sundance juries as well. The popular *The Brothers McMullen*, the Grand Jury Prize winner in 1995, was apparently a compromise choice after the jury split on other, more rarefied choices. Back in 1990, the jury gave its top prize to the formidably inaccessible *Chameleon Street*, giving a lesser award to a tremendous film that could have benefited from the buzz of being number one, Charles Burnett's *To Sleep with Anger*.

One way Sundance has managed to keep the competition safe for orphan films is by ghettoizing established independent directors in the Premiers section. But given that these directors are still at a disadvantage in the real movie world, no matter how heroic they seem in Park City, wouldn't it make sense to practice a form of cinematic triage and allow films that have a chance to succeed in megaplexes to benefit from the imprimatur of being a Sundance winner and not focus so lovingly on those that are D.O.A.?

Sundance has also looked askance at other films with audience potential, either rejecting them outright or putting them in the less prestigious American Spectrum section. Wes Anderson's *Bottle Rocket* and Carl Franklin's *One False Move*, both independent landmarks, were rejected, and *Gods and Monsters*, good enough to earn an Oscar for best adapted screenplay, was deemed not strong enough for the competition and relegated to Spectrum.

Sundance has thrived because it has shown that there is a market for the best of these films; it has shown that Americans will flock to hand-crafted, non-machine-made independent cinema if it is well done. Commercial vitality is not an enemy or a danger sign; it's something to be embraced.

Similarly, supporting films whose potential audience is microscopic, worshiping their inevitable lack of success like a relic of the true cross, is both perversely holding onto something outmoded in the world Sundance has created and missing the chance to do more tangible good.

To its credit, Sundance seems to be trying to change. The 2000 event was, in terms of overall quality and the lack of hair-pulling fiascoes, the most successful festival in memory. The pleasantly schizophrenic interaction between the minions of Hollywood and the scruffy independent world shows no sign of disappearing and continues to prove the truth of the familiar dictum that what doesn't kill makes one stronger. And no matter what else changes, this festival can't help but remain the place where dreams come true. "It's in the nature of hope," director Allie Light said in 1994 after winning the Freedom of Expression award for her *Dialogues with Madwomen*, "that the more you put it down, the more it seems to rise like a wild dream." If you want to find a credo for Sundance, you couldn't do better than that.

ShoWest

LAS VEGAS — In a plaid shirt, loose-fitting pants, and nonchalant attitude, Adam Sandler was indistinguishable from the fans who've made him one of the most sought-after stars in America. "I'm not particularly smart," he mock-confessed to increasing laughter and applause. "I'm not particularly talented; I'm not particularly good looking. But I'm a multimillionaire because of you people. So thank you very much."

Welcome to ShoWest, as in show me the talent, show me a little respect, and, most of all, show me the money. Again and again at the awards banquet of an event that's been called everything from "the largest and most important gathering of motion picture professionals in the world" to simply "the greatest show on earth," the gratitude expressed by Sandler, named ShoWest Comedy Star of the Year, was echoed by some of the biggest movie stars around.

Here was Sean Connery, talking up his next film, *Entrapment*, and concluding with a heartfelt hope "that we'll make a lot of money." Here was Meg Ryan wryly confessing, "I've never been called 'bankable' in front of so many people." Here was Bobby Farrelly, half of *There's Something about Mary*'s Farrelly brothers, admitting, in a serious moment for him, "If it weren't for you people, Pete and I would be doing TV." And here was superpopular Will Smith, introduced by director Barry

Sonnenfeld as the "ShoWest Human Being of the Planet," topping the Farrellys with the deadpan tribute, "Without you, someone else would have had to buy the building and put movie theaters in there."

On one level, ShoWest, which had all these stars and more as its twenty-fifth anniversary guests, is simply a convention, a film festival if you like, for people who own movie theaters both in this country and overseas. Delegate registration is capped at 3,600, but when friends, family, and related personnel are added in, an estimated 10–12,000 people annually crowd Bally's hotel/casino complex in the center of the Las Vegas strip.

ShoWest is a place where awards are given, like the one that went to Charles D. Cretors, a fourth-generation popcorn man whose great-grandfather patented the process of popping corn in oil back in 1885. It's a place where trade announcements are made by the National Association of Theater Owners (NATO for short, and jokingly thanked a few years back by Leslie Nielsen for "the wonderful job you're doing in Bosnia"), which recently unveiled a new initiative to keep the audio level of coming attractions trailers down. And it's a place where speeches can lapse into boilerplate phraseology like "return on capital," "cash flow perspective," and the always popular "ancillary revenue streams." Unlike other festivals (no names, please), the people here are not frightened by the prospect of earning a little money.

ShoWest in fact has a language of its own, opaque to civilians. Theater owners are known as exhibitors ("'exhibitionists,' as we call them in England," Hugh Grant joked). Movie studios are never called studios, but are rather broken down into their component parts: production, the process of making films, and its more significant partner, distribution, the system of getting them into theaters. Moviegoers are often (no kidding) called guests, and as for the concession stand, it's inevitably referred to, with appropriate reverence, as "our profit center."

So calling ShoWest merely a convention is like calling *The Blair Witch Project* a satisfactory earner. ShoWest is the place where George Lucas, not known to be passionate about public speaking, came to give exhibitors "a special big hug" for their efforts with the *Star Wars* reissue and to personally unveil the new coming attractions trailer for *The Phantom Menace*. It's the place that Miramax's Harvey Weinstein flew to from New York not to receive an award, not even to present an award, but just to present a presenter to the assembled multitudes. And the very last creative thing Stanley Kubrick did on this planet was to personally put together a thirty-second teaser for *Eyes Wide Shut*, his first film in more than a decade, specifically for the ShoWest crowd.

Though little known to the public, the four-day ShoWest extravaganza turns out to be in many ways the most fascinating, even the most significant dawn-to-dusk movie event in the country, drawing correspondents not only from expected sources like *Entertainment Weekly* and *Premier* but *Time*, *Newsweek*, and major newspapers as well. If you want to know what's happening in mainstream moviemaking and moviegoing today, this is the place to be. "If you're not here," a conventioneer told the *Hollywood Reporter* a few years back, "you're not in business."

A privileged look behind the scenes at the interlocking gears of the theatrical experience, ShoWest has increased in importance over twenty-five years in part because it's several events in one. One part is hard-core educational, a presentation of in-depth statistics, surveys, and information. One part is flashy, an energizing showcase where studios display what they hope theaters will be showing in the months ahead. Perhaps the most irresistible segment is the trade show, where more than 500 vendors pack booths with an eye toward selling every single thing you can think of that a movie theater might possibly want or need, and some, like the tiny ice cream pellets frozen to 40 degrees below zero and dubbed "Dippin' Dots," that it would be difficult to even imagine.

To come to ShoWest as more or less a civilian, as a once and future moviegoer, is to understand that in our lives inside theaters we've all been living a "Truman Show" experience without ever knowing it. Every casual decision we make, from what to see to what to eat, has been carefully observed, analyzed, and acted upon. As a top Nestle marketing official put it when discussing strong consumer feelings about high concession prices, "I don't want to say they can be manipulated, but they can be affected."

ShoWest, obviously, hasn't always been this big, and it hasn't always been in Las Vegas either. It started with a 1974 meeting at Los Angeles International Airport between three key figures in West Coast theatrical distribution, Jerry Forman, Bob Selig, and B. V. Sturdivant. Differences of opinion with the national organization meant that California exhibitors were not then members of NATO and, remembers Forman, head of Pacific Theaters, "We were trying to establish a forum and a place to meet, to bring exhibition and distribution together in a little trade show where you could have a couple of lunches and just open an informal dialogue."

The first ShoWest (no one is sure anymore just who came up with the name) was held in San Diego in 1975. The attendance was roughly 200, there were barely more than a dozen booths at the trade show, the filmmaking companies who attended were mostly marginal entities like Brut Productions and Crown International, and the big news was the new Containment Screen for drive-in theaters, which for the first time did not deflect images out onto the highway. "That," said William Kartozian, later president of NATO, chuckling at the memory, "shows where we've come in twenty-five years."

If there is one key to how big ShoWest has become it was the decision, starting with the 1979 event, to move the proceedings to Las Vegas, a city where the airport looks like a casino and the casinos look like an Egyptian pyramid (Luxor), a medieval castle (Excalibur), even the Manhattan skyline (New York, New York). The whole city can be viewed as one big show, and the synergy between location and event couldn't have been more promising.

Like the movies, Las Vegas is about money and entertainment, about using dazzling fantasy to make you feel good about parting with your dollars. It's a place where everything conspires to make a mockery out of will power, where towering water fountains are choreographed to Frank Sinatra singing "Luck Be a Lady Tonight," and ads suggest that those in a matrimonial frame of mind "have your wedding ceremony in our luxurious helicopter over Las Vegas. A unique and special way to begin your marriage."

Vegas is "the key to the whole event," said a top distribution executive, a potent energy source for the convention and a place, when all is said and done, where movie people feel right at home. "It's pretty glamorous, there's a whole exciting aura about Las Vegas," says Jean Gregory, who runs the Deluxe Outdoor Theaters in Clermont, Indiana. "If the convention was held somewhere else, there wouldn't be as many people attending." In 1989 the national organization finally got the message, and ShoWest, which had been run since its inception by NATO of California/Nevada, became the official convention of the entire exhibition industry as well.

Also attracted to Las Vegas were international exhibitors, theater owners in far-off places like Thailand and Brazil, who felt even more removed from the heart of the business than their counterparts on the outskirts of Indianapolis. They came from so many countries — more than forty were counted in 1999 — that ShoWest set aside its first day just for them. And their problems.

Who knew, for instance, that video piracy is so out of control in Vietnam and Malaysia that the exhibition business has become close to impossible. Or that Russia, a nation of 170 million, "has virtually no modern screens." Or that Italy suffers in the summer from a lack of air-conditioned theaters, and that British exhibitors sometimes have show times dictated by bossy local governments.

ShoWest can't solve these difficulties, of course, but it can offer a forum to schmooze and complain and feel among friends. American exhibitors tend to patronize ShoWest for the same reasons; as a theater owner tartly put it to the *Hollywood Reporter*, "You're with your peers, the people you love and the people you hate."

There is an additional lure, of course, and that is the glamour, the chance to witness movie celebrity in the flesh, to experience what NATO's Kartozian calls "treating them to a bit of Hollywood in Las Vegas."

Does it work? You bet. "We like to see the stars of the films we run in person," says Daniel Van Orden, circuit general manager of the Fulton, Missouri–based B&B Theaters, which owns two dozen screens in that state and neighboring Kansas. "It makes for good talk in small towns."

The studios, ever solicitous, have tried to oblige, putting on elaborate luncheons and dinners where wave after wave of stars parade to the dais and smile at exhibitors and a slickly produced montage of coming attractions (known as a product reel) is screened. Warner Bros. has traditionally set the standard for these events, and its dais can groan under the accumulated celebrity of Clint Eastwood, Keanu Reeves, Will Smith, Salma Hayek, Hugh Grant, Jeanne Tripplehorn, Elizabeth Hurley, George Clooney, Cuba Gooding, Jr., Geoffrey Rush, and numerous others. They're all flown in on company jets in a hectic undertaking that *Premier* called "kamikaze publicity" and Tom Hanks characterized as "one of the great and goofy twenty-four hours you get to spend in the business."

But even though ShoWest picks up the tab for food at these events, providing that touch of glamour has proved expensive and difficult for studios. Those jets from around the world cost serious money, as does paying for a stop in production for whatever films the stars happen to be in at the moment. When all the expenses are added in, one of these afternoons can cost a studio one or even two million dollars.

So it's not surprising, especially in a world where the top ten movie circuits control 60 percent of America's theatrical gross, that the studios periodically chafe at the expense of the ShoWest experience and search for alternatives. In 1995, for instance, MGM/UA flew thirty-two top exhibition executives to Paris for a preview experience. Even Warners, one of ShoWest's most faithful supporters, now cites expense in its plan to do the Las Vegas event only every other year.

Given the expense and difficulty, why do the studios do it at all? In addition to intangible factors like inertia and the value of showing the flag to the industry, studios value the kind of instant feedback on upcoming product that only showing it to thousands of people who have a major stake in a film's success or failure can provide. The feeling was unanimous — and accurate — after the New Line luncheon, for instance, that the new Mike Myers movie, *Austin Powers: The Spy Who Shagged Me*, was the likeliest success on that studio's roster, and Warner Bros. watchers had the same dead-on sense about *The Matrix* and the Tom Hanks–starring, Stephen King–based *Green Mile*.

But while these successes may have been expected, ShoWest sometimes provides the more valuable service of anointing unexpected films. "Studios might not even be sure themselves what they've got, and ShoWest show-cases what might be sleeper product," explains Barry Reardon, Warners' highly respected former head of distribution. "All of a sudden, boom, an unheralded film like *Free Willy* can become a big hit here." Reardon put a more colorful spin on the same thought when he told a reporter a few years back, "A little picture can get kosher at ShoWest."

Also, as more and more of the mainstream media cover ShoWest, the event becomes a perfect opportunity to create valuable international publicity and put studio spin on a film. Which is just what Warners did by providing a small but provocative (and, as it turned out, misleading) glimpse of Kubrick's *Eyes Wide Shut*, characterized by *Daily Variety* as "an eye-opening teaser that features more explicit nude footage of Nicole Kidman than the entire Broadway run of *The Blue Room*."

As important as the information the clips provide, the ShoWest stu-dio events, where executives are dutifully paraded onto the dais like members of the old Soviet Politburo, are useful in fostering a kind of intimacy and camaraderie between exhibitors and distributors, a cele-bratory "among ourselves" atmosphere capable of creating good feeling that can last through an entire year.

Watching Cuba Gooding, Jr., juggling pats of butter at the Warner Bros. luncheon, seeing Will Smith mock-shine cochairman Terry Semel's shoes (don't ask), hearing Smith unexpectedly extol the virtues of Tucks Medicated Comfort Pads ("I sure hope we did a tie-in with that company," Semel commented), and hearing George Clooney say that he and *Boogie Nights*'s Mark Wahlberg were "stopping at Planet Hollywood to drop off Mark's penis," exhibitors were certainly well on the way to being convinced they were as much a part of the Warners family as Clint Eastwood, candidly introduced by Semel as "the reason we can pay the bills."

In case exhibitors don't get the underlying message that the studios think they're important, a lot of specific making nice and stroking of theater owners goes on at ShoWest. A few years ago, Julia Roberts, the biggest of female stars, assured the ShoWest crowd that her hair in *My Best Friend's Wedding* was "red and long and curly, just the way you like it." In 1999, Peter Cherin, president of News Corp., Twentieth Century Fox's parent corporation, showed up to call film "the greatest igniter of human emotions ever invented" and promise that "the movies will always remain the core priority of what we do." This mutual admiration society is authentic: both exhibition and distribution unwaveringly believe that a good film is a film that makes money, period, and this willingness to speak the same language when it comes to evaluating product is one both sides cherish.

Though it doesn't draw the big stars, even the informational/ educational aspect of ShoWest can seem glamorous in the right hands. AC Nielsen EDI, for instance, enlivened the statistics in its new Movie*Views survey of national moviegoing habits by using colorful graphics and making the frequent moviegoers who drive the marketplace (the 18 percent of ticket buyers who account for 66 percent of the box office gross) sound like the stars of their own TV program about poundage-challenged individuals by calling them "The Heavies." Among the more daunting pieces of information revealed were that reviews were important to only 9 percent of all respondents (but 12 percent cent of The Heavies!) and that 82 percent of moviegoers had no clue as to which studio released *Titanic*.

Easily the most entertaining of the information providers was the venerable Jack Valenti, chairman of the Motion Picture Association of America, who made the annual state-of-the-industry presentation. At least as interesting as Valenti's news that production costs had stayed pretty much the same while marketing and distribution numbers had jumped a daunting 13 percent was the chairman's gift for stem-winding

oratorical flourishes. Looking as if he would have been just as comfortable wearing a toga on the floor of the Senate of Rome, the silver-haired
Valenti made it sound natural to call high costs "that fiscal Godzilla
slouching around movie budgets for so long, like a sullen, unwelcome
Banquo's ghost." He enlivened things further with references to what
happened when the Saracens invaded France in the eighth century,
causing NATO's Kartozian to comment, "It's rare to get an account of the
Saracen invasion from an eyewitness."

While theater owners seemed baffled by futurist Kevin R. Roche, who
insisted that the line between entertainment and retail was blurring and
that in the twenty-first century competition would not be over market
share but over "capturing share of mind, share of time," they paid a lot
more attention to seminars on two of the biggest issues facing them in
the here-and-now, the explosion of the megaplex phenomenon, a.k.a.
"megaplex mania," and the maturing of digital technology.

Roughly defined as a theater with from a dozen to thirty-something
screens, the megaplex was virtually unheard of just a few years ago. Even
the now-déclassé multiplex is a relatively new phenomenon, and it was
as recently as the late 1950s that exhibitor Stanley Durwood, head of the
AMC chain and considered the creator of the duplex, realized when he
closed the balcony during the third week of "a crummy picture" he was
running at the Roxy in Kansas City that "if I had another crummy picture upstairs, I could double the gross."

Today, the megaplex is where everyone wants to be: forty-one of the
fifty top grossing theaters in America are megaplexes. They are enormous enterprises, as big as 150,000 square feet, utilizing 4,000 light
bulbs to illuminate six-story lobby rotundas, and they seat 12–15,000
people on a given weekend day, between two and three million in a year.
Yet they've also caused havoc in the exhibition sector, making non-
megaplexes seem out of date years before their time, "siphoning customers from existing theaters," said Mike Campbell, head of Regal
Cinemas, the nation's largest chain, in what proved to be an accurate
warning, "like a huge vacuum cleaner and cannibalizing their business."

These behemoths can be daunting to run, with even veteran theater managers saying they were not prepared for what they saw. So in addition to informal discussions of these issues, ShoWest provided a nuts and bolts event called "Managing Top Grossing Megaplexes" laden with real-world specifics. "You have to know who touches the money," said one manager, detailing his own "triple-check system." Another talked of how disoriented customers may become because of a megaplex's size and described authorizing his staff to "take ownership" of anyone within their physical "zone of influence" and solve any problem within that space. Plus, you have to be smart with your concessions, said John King, Jr., general manager of the Winnetka 21 in Chatsworth, California, relating how an exclusive contract to serve Pink's hot dogs, the pride of Hollywood, led to 175,000 sold in the first year, a figure that drew appreciative gasps from the savvy crowd.

The other much discussed issue at ShoWest was the coming of digital technology and whether, as one speaker put it, "we will enter the new millennium embracing a 100-year-old technology or a new one." Two companies put on side-by-side comparisons of their digital images with Kodak film, and while the general consensus was that film still had the edge, it was a near thing. Later that same day, George Lucas stunned the crowd by announcing that *The Phantom Menace* would play in four theaters in a digital version and that he'd shoot the next *Star Wars* prequel exclusively with digital equipment. Said one exhibitor to the *Hollywood Reporter*, "The sound you heard during the *Star Wars* trailer was twenty guys from Kodak jumping off the roof of the hotel."

. . .

1 box Clark Miniatures
1 box Sour Patch assorted candy
1 box Hot Tamales ("Great Cinnamon Taste!")
    chewy cinnamon-flavored candies
1 box Nuclear Sqworms ("You'll Really Dig 'Em!")
    sour neon Gummi Worms

1 bag microwave popcorn from Packaging Concepts
    Inc., "Converters of Flexible Packaging"
1 bag Strips for Dips tortilla chips from Ricos,
    "Originators of Nachos in Concessions"
1 bag theater-style tortilla chips from Wyandot
    World Class Snacks
1 bag Starburst fruit chews
1 box BC's Candy-Coated Real Milk Chocolate Pieces
    from Banner Candy ("Banner Makes Movies Magic")
    to celebrate their 70th anniversary
1 sack Swiss-Miss French Vanilla Cappuccino
    ("Just Add Hot Water") instant coffee blend
1 bag Care Bears Gummi Bears
    ("Made with Real Fruit Juice")
1 bag Nestle Raisinets
1 package Star Punch artificially flavored
    strawberry licorice
1 package Funacho Zesty Cheese Sauce
1 package Ricos Nacho Cheese Dip
    ("Spiced Right! Good Hot–or Cold!")

> *— edible contents of concessions bag*
> *given to every ShoWest delegate*

.   .   .

They call it simply "the trade show," but if there is a secret heart to the
ShoWest experience, it lies in this sprawling, 541-booth extravaganza
squeezed into a specially constructed 90,000-square-foot tent perched in
Bally's backyard. It's a cradle-to-grave tour, in a manner of speaking, of
the theater-going experience, from Wagner, the company that invented
the slotted marquee letter in the 1920s to consultants like the Plotkin
Group who help you hire the help ("Reduce employee theft and
turnover! Identify honest, dependable, hardworking, capable employees!") to a seat refurbisher named Premier with the motto "We Do for
Theater Seating What Tarantino Did for Travolta."

It's at the trade show that you can meet the legendary Frank Liberto

of Ricos Products of San Antonio, the genial man credited with origi-
nating what's known as "concession nachos," a Tex-Mex snack that he's
introduced to twenty-three countries. Here, not unlike the open bazaar
in Ouagadougou, Burkina Faso, hypnotic waves of committed salespeo-
ple call out beseechingly as you wander the aisles, and even the woman
who hands out sacks emblazoned with the Coke logo insists "they're not
empty, they're filled with air, absolutely essential for life."

Because theaters make a sizable part of their profits from the concession stand (most of the box office revenue goes back to the studios, especially in a film's busy opening weeks), it's this aspect of the theatrical
experience that draws the most vendors and the most interest. Some
half-a-dozen popcorn-related enterprises, for instance, including the
makers of Popwise Popping Oil ("Your Popcorn's Ready for an Oil
Change"), compete in this high-profile area, and if you want to understand how the Metric Weight Volume Tester (MWVT for short) measures
all-important kernel expansion, this is the place to learn. Also on hand
and prepared to talk up their products were salesmen for Jelly Bellys
("making 40 million of these beans a day keeps us busy"), Cookie Dough
Bites ("people can't say no to cookie dough"), and Knott's Berry Farm
Smoothies with names like Fiji Freeze and Strawberry Goes Bananas
("zero to awesome in twenty seconds.")

No one here is without a story, like Josh Schreider and Bryan
Freeman of Bavarian Brothers Pretzel Bakery ("Twisted at Birth") in
Van Nuys. No, they're not brothers, they're not even Bavarian, but they
are passionate about pretzels. "We started this company on credit cards,"
Schreider says, his eyes hot with pretzel fervor. "We bought a pretzel-
making machine from a junkyard owner who said it couldn't be made to
work. I took it apart; there were thousands of pieces on the back room
floor of a pizza parlor, and the owner bet me I couldn't put it together
again." And today? "Over the past seven months, we've been doubling
the number of theaters we're in every twenty-three days." Is this a great
country, or what?

It's also, regrettably, a messy country, and ShoWest does not stint on cleaning opportunities. Arnold Meltzer of Ampac Theater Cleaning Services talked of finding everything from underwear to sleeping people to an Uzi machine gun on the floors of theaters, while brothers Jaimy and Dameon Johnson of Inglewood demonstrated the Kwick Bag trash container, which fits conveniently under theater seats. And Kory Wright of Natural Solutions Cleaning Productions ("The Nation's Leading Producer of Human-Friendly, Building-Friendly, Environment-Friendly Conscious Cleaning Products") boasted, "If you drink this product, which employees will, it won't kill them."

A veteran of more than a dozen ShoWests is Robert Hotch, president of Modular Hardware, which specializes in toilet partitions, hardware, and accessories, and he, too, has a spiel: "Everyone who goes to movie theaters ends up in the bathroom. More people rate the movie theater by the condition of the bathroom than anything else."

This logic worked on a theater owner from the nation of Georgia that Hotch met at ShoWest a year or so back. "Not only did he order the partitions and hardware, we had to send him the paper and soap. He can't get it over there. Needless to say, the money was in the bank before we sent it, and in American dollars, not rubles."

All of this energetic selling can be exhausting, and the trade show also offered mini-massages ranging from the $5 Feel Good to the $30 Ultimate from a group called On-Site Stress Relief, Inc. But for this visitor, at least, there was something inescapably exhilarating about this kind of joyful cacophony. Movie theaters are where it all began, where everyone first fell in love with movies, simply but finally, and if that love still endures, what ShoWest has to offer is easy to embrace wholeheartedly. Somewhere in the world, it's show time every minute of every day, and what could be better than that?

PART TWO

Festivals with Geopolitical Agendas

FESPACO

OUAGADOUGOU, BURKINA FASO — The crowd, estimated at 40,000, pours through an honor guard of mounted camels and overflows the biggest stadium in the country. For the next three and a half hours a kaleidoscopic spectacle unfolds, made up of flowery political speeches in two languages, performances by celebrated musicians like Malhatini and the Mahotela Queens, a pantomime executed by five hundred schoolchidren, choreographed prancing by elaborately costumed horsemen, dazzling fireworks, even a ceremonial ribbon-cutting and release of multicolored balloons by the nation's president.

Is this any way to open a film festival? For FESPACO, the Festival Panafricaine du Cinéma de Ouagadougou, a spectacular occasion whose fourteenth edition took place in 1995, it is simply business as usual.

Held every other year at the end of February, FESPACO's celebration of African cinema (an event relatively unknown in this country despite visits by domestic celebrities like Alice Walker, Tracy Chapman, and John Singleton) is an extravaganza with few peers, a massive cultural happening that shreds preconceived notions of festivals as merely places where tickets are taken and movies are shown.

Yes, there are films. Hundreds of them from all across Africa and the African diaspora are available to be seen here, both on the big screen and in a parallel video film market known as MICA, providing an unequaled opportunity to view the entire range of production from Algeria to South Africa and beyond.

The choicest films at FESPACO compete for the festival's equivalent of Cannes's Palme d'Or, the Etalon (Stallion) de Yennenga, named after the legendary horsewoman who is considered the progenitor of the country's predominant Mossi tribe. And all entries are hugely appreciated by the legendarily responsive African audiences, one of FESPACO's lures, crowds who pack the theaters and roar appreciatively at situations that strike home.

"In the United States, African films are shown in the context of museums and art cinema, so they tend to be received reverently, with deference and respect," explained Richard Peña, program director for the Film Society of Lincoln Center, director of the New York Film Festival, and a FESPACO visitor. "Here you can see how open and dialogic the relationship to film is. Godard said that cinema is what goes on between the screen and the audience, and it really goes on here. You are seeing a truly communal experience."

But more than for what it shows, FESPACO is noteworthy as a matter of enormous national pride for this striving West African country the size of Colorado. Called "desperately, and famously, poor" by one guide book, "not near the top of anyone's short list of travel destinations" by another, French West Africa's former Upper Volta, in a scenario that even Hollywood would reject as outlandish, has managed by a combination of passion and determination to turn itself into the undisputed capital of the African film world.

Ouaga, as the locals call this hot, dusty city of half a million, gives itself over body and soul to FESPACO, starting with releasing all its fifteen screens to the festival. These range from the spacious, air-conditioned Ciné Neerwaya (meaning "the beauty has come" in Moré, the primary local language), at 1,200 seats one of the biggest theaters in West Africa, to outdoor venues in the city's remoter locales that are more prosaically named ("Secteur 17," "Secteur 29") after the areas they're located in.

I arrived in the city, as most international visitors do, in the cooler nighttime. Though Ouaga has so little electrical illumination that a well-lit Elf gas station stood out like a spaceship, what was most noticeable during the drive into town from the airport was the conviviality of the street life, how many people were out and about. Also noticeable, not to say unavoidable, was the multiplicity of motorbikes, called Mobylettes after the most popular brand, whose taillights twinkled like fireflies in the pleasantly sultry night air.

Though the bikes, the city's most popular vehicle, are even more omnipresent during the day, Ouaga when the sun is out is in some ways a different story. Because Burkina is part of the edge-of-the-Sahara area known as the Sahel (from the Arabic word for shore), it is a famously hot and dusty place for much of the year, so dry it is rare to see a Westerner without a bottle of Lafi, the local mineral water.

Yet unlike neighboring Abidjan, the bustling capital of the Ivory Coast, Ouaga has the refreshing air of an overgrown village, with few billboards, no skyscrapers to speak of, and the ambiance of a city under construction that might never be finished. The streets are either completely nameless or grandly dedicated to heroes of liberation like Nelson Mandela, Che Guevara, and Kwame Nkruma. And just a ten-minute journey into the countryside brings you to traditional village compounds that look as they have for centuries.

Though Burkina is a poor country, it is an industrious one, with makeshift market stalls seen on many Ouaga streets. The intensity and variety of commercial life include a steady parade of women dressed in colorful print dresses balancing huge loads of everything from oranges to piles of mirrors on their heads. And bicycles do not just transport people, they convey towers of hay, massive water cisterns, sacks of coal, piles of ox skins, anything and everything you might not even imagine could be moved this way. Even my French-speaking driver would occasionally eye a particularly outrageous load and sigh, "Ah, Afrique."

At the same time, it is impossible to move through Ouaga without noticing the poverty, visible in everything from persistent child beggars (often sent out by Islamic imams) to grim housing to the country's paper money, which has been worn to a remarkable thinness by repeated use. And the city's ever-present vultures, visible everywhere and often just perched on buildings to have a look around, do not make for a prosperous feeling.

Yet talking about Ouaga in terms of what it lacks gives a misleading impression of the city. For in line with the cliché of African travel that you go to the East for the wildlife and the West for the people, the Burkinabe are known for their wonderful spirit. Warm, lively, with an enviable self-assurance linked to a dignified sense of who they are, the citizens of Ouaga have no intention of being defined by their poverty and manage to turn almost every transaction with them into a restorative experience.

FESPACO makes itself felt locally in numerous ways. Those who can afford it wear clothing made from special FESPACO commemorative cloth, the national lottery has inaugurated a special "Millionaire" drawing to mark the festival, postage stamps have been issued to honor Gaston Kaboré and Idrissa Ouedraogo, the country's most celebrated living directors, and one visiting film critic unexpectedly found himself chatting about movies in a private audience with Burkina's president.

Several of the city's main streets, festooned with banners proclaiming uplifting slogans like "FESPACO: Pride of a Continent," are closed off and turned into a pedestrian shopping mall generically called Rue Marchande. There Ouaga's residents, benefiting from a government decree giving everyone half days off for the duration of the festival, jostle with tourists at crowded booths where merchants from all over Africa sell souvenirs, hand out free cigarettes and condoms (AIDS is a major problem here as in the rest of the continent), and distribute literature about buying fax machines and supporting the Intra-African Union for Human Rights.

There is also the city's Grand Marché, a reinforced concrete structure in the center of town that is one of West Africa's newest, and reportedly one of the cleanest and most manageable as well. Its sights and smells are immediately overwhelming, with everything from slabs of salt and piles of dried fish to gorgeous fabric and imported Chicago Bulls T-shirts on sale from innumerable tiny booths on several different levels.

If you slow down just to think about a purchase, or even if you don't, determined sellers importune you in French and occasionally English and don't hesitate to follow you to other booths, talking furiously. Once buying is a possibility, bargaining is essential: to agree to the first offered price is unthinkable, like rushing right to the table at a dinner party without first saying hello to your host. Bargaining has everything to do with ritual and tradition and almost nothing to do with gouging money out of the unwary, so much so that resident foreigners who gain a reputation for agreeing to the first offered price and refusing to bargain are considered undesirable customers. And should you indicate that your French is weak, the seller, even if he looks as if he had stepped out of the Arabian Nights, is sure to reach into his voluminous robes and come out with a pocket calculator to help things along.

For those without the inclination to shop, international exhibitions on the art of the Niger Valley and the image of Africa in Europe were available during the festival I attended. And devotees of nightlife who didn't plan on showing up for FESPACO's 8 A.M. press screenings could partake of the "Nuits Chaudes" or "Hot Nights" series of dance concerts that didn't even get started till around midnight.

As for the city's more conventional tourist attractions, they tended to be slighted during the festival. This proved especially true at the Musée National, located inside the Lycée Bogodogo on Avenue d'Oubritenga headed out of town, where I was the only visitor in an oppressively steamy building. None of this fazed Jean-Pierre Bikienga, the museum's guide, who took me on a passionate, detailed tour of the collection's masks and artifacts, delivered in a musical French that was pleasant to the ear and easy to understand.

My favorite item was a gris-gris sack confiscated by police after the arrest of a potent local sorcerer accused of using magic to kill his enemies. The sack had initially been hung on a branch of a blooming tree, which proceeded to sicken and die within days. Afterward the sack had been left outside in the heat and rain for a year before it was considered safe to touch. It did look considerably the worse for wear, but the sinister air about it continued to be unmistakable.

Yet even all this does not tell the whole story of FESPACO. It doesn't explain why the festival draws thousands of journalists and participants from dozens of countries as distant as Japan, Romania, and Brazil as well as African luminaries who in 1995 ranged from Nigeria's Nobel Prize–winning novelist Wole Soyinka to the controversial South African political figure Winnie Mandela, then on her first state visit to West Africa.

Simply put, FESPACO has become the preeminent African cultural event of any kind. To stand in the lobby of the Hotel Independence, the festival's central meeting place, to admire the various styles of traditional dress and read the gazetteer of countries on passing name tags is to feel that the entire continent has somehow gathered in this one place. For the eight days it occupies, FESPACO is the focal point of Africa's consciousness, the place where this perennially neglected continent comes to examine itself. And as the medium chosen for this task, film assumes an importance that is rarely felt elsewhere.

"Our country is modest and underdeveloped, and people used to say that priority in development should be for agriculture and other things," says Filippe Sawadogo, at that time FESPACO's affably driven secretary general and the man who ran the festival for more than a decade. "Now we understand that no people can be developed without their own culture, that showing our own culture is a priority. If you know yourself in terms of identity, you can succeed."

The year 1995, celebrated worldwide as the centenary of cinema, seemed especially promising for Africa. Both the Toronto Film Festival and the British Film Institute used FESPACO as the occasion to announce major new African film series for later that year, and the general consensus was that, in Richard Peña's words, "African film feels vibrant at a time when so much of cinema is looking around at how to cut its losses.

A wonderful and intoxicating sense of pride hangs over the whole festival, you feel nothing but hope here."

Though the postcolonial history of African cinema is no more than thirty-something years old, the medium has always been one of enormous importance for this continent, partly because the reality that, in one director's words, "there are no illiterates in the world of cinema" makes it the ideal method for reaching the widest possible audience.

More than that, Africans feel an intense need to control the way both their own people and the world at large view the African experience. "Traditionally images have been used to dominate Africa, doing damage to the minds of colonized people, telling them they are less important," says Gaston Kaboré, the pioneering Burkinabe director whose *Wend Kuuni* is celebrated as the first black African picture to win a César for the best Francophone film. "But ever since we started making films, we have used cinema as a tool of liberation, liberating the individual in his mind. We need to describe our own reality by ourselves."

Though this is a feeling that echoes across the entire continent, there are other factors that divide African filmmakers, and none more sharply than the language issue. For reasons that are still debated, perhaps stemming from the French belief in culture as an end in itself versus an English desire to make all things utilitarian, the majority of the most successful and celebrated directors in Africa come from the Francophone countries of the West and the North.

As a result, FESPACO has in the past been viewed as a Francophone event, where it is the rare film that has English subtitles and eleven of the twelve winners of the Etalon through 1995 have come from countries where French is the predominant European language. But though the French continue to provide considerable assistance to West African filmmakers, the festival has taken increasing steps to make itself accessible to English speakers, and in 1995, with South Africa invited to attend for the first time, even more of an attempt at outreach in terms of simultaneous translation and bilingual printed material was made. "We are not Francophone or Anglophone," said FESPACO's Sawadogo on opening night. "We are Africaphone."

For the filmmakers themselves, who come to the festival by the hundreds, these kinds of divisions seem less important than the rare chance to mingle with peers. Though admitting that "non-French speakers can tend to feel out of it," prominent Nigerian director Ola Balogun said that that drawback was far outweighed by "the unique opportunity to see other filmmakers. It's not like we are all living in one country; we are dispersed, with different schedules to cope with, so there are lots of reunions here."

Because of its importance, even the most celebrated African directors try not to miss the festival. The 1995 jury president, the celebrated seventy-one-year-old Ousmane Sembene, called "l'aîné des anciens (the elder of elders)," considers it a duty never to skip a festival, and Burkina's Idrissa Ouedraogo warmly calls FESPACO "my first mother, the place I made my first short film for."

In fact, FESPACO has gotten so big and successful that, in an unexpected parallel to the controversy that eternally swirls around America's Sundance Film Festival, participants argue about whether the event has gotten too large and too commercial, whether it has lost its Africanness, its sense of direction, the purity of its spirit.

"People grumble that as FESPACO has gotten bigger it has grown out of all proportion to the growth of African cinema," says June Givanni, the British Film Institute's chief African film programmer. "But it is a celebration, and I don't think those things are necessarily bad. The festival has the difficult task of balancing things, but you can still find the whole spectrum here, the edge and the passionate discussions with people not mincing words as well as the glitzy side."

What most African filmmakers wanted to talk about, however, was not FESPACO's flaws but the perennial allied difficulties of first raising money to make a film and then, something that turns out to be even more difficult, finding a way to get it shown on the African continent.

Because one of the great paradoxes of African filmmaking is that, in

Gaston Kaboré's words, "Our films are strangers in their own territories. It is easier to watch an African film in New York, Los Angeles, London or Paris than in Lesotho, Botswana, Nigeria or Kenya. If audiences are given the opportunity to see them, they are rushing to go, African audiences are keen to watch movies where their reality is reflected. But our films are made outside of an economic system, we do not have producers or distributors with financial and economic clout, so our movies do not have the ability to circulate."

NINETY PERCENT OF AFRICAN FILMS WILL NEVER BE SEEN BY AFRICANS THEMSELVES. So reads a flyer handed out by Daniel Cuxac, whose Ivory Coast–based DC Productions is one of the few companies attempting to put African films on video to increase their local availability. "After FES-PACO the light will be off and we will find again the hard realities," he says. "After their films are shown in the festivals, the filmmakers stay in their houses, they don't know where to go." Language barriers, the expense of subtitles, the uncertainty of getting both money and films back from other countries all contribute to the problem.

One potential way out of these difficulties, at least for the most prominent directors, is to get financing from European entities like television networks, usually French but increasingly German, Dutch, and British as well. But taking this money, welcome as it is, can present its own set of problems.

"When you write a script to please European producers, you take their expectations into consideration; if you are spending ten million French francs, you are wondering what kind of box office results you will get in France," Gaston Kaboré explained to me. "Our films can become unbalanced, we are so weak we are turning like this and like that. The danger is forgetting your own people, your own fundamental vision, and presenting Africa only as Europe is prepared to receive it. The danger is we will lose our souls."

Four years later, Africa's Francophone filmmakers were, if anything, more concerned. Senegalese-born director Mama Keita told *Variety* in May 1999 that he was "really worried that the image we are seeing of

Africa in most films has virtually nothing to do with the reality of the individual countries.

"Even if you look at the French government funds, which are supposed to help develop African cinema," Keita added, "what happens is the cash goes to pay French technicians, French laboratories and French post-production facilities, who all work on African films. The money stays in France. Why do you think there are no post-production facilities worth speaking of in Francophone Africa?"

Besides lamenting requirements from funding companies that the film be shot in Africa — "that means you can't use the money if you are an African director who wants to do a film about the African experience in France" — Keita also noted that "many of the political regimes in Francophone Africa are not exactly democracies. You are not going to be allowed to shoot a film about what life is really like. That's why the African film today boils down to shots of naked kids running around mud-hut villages. That doesn't bother anybody."

One filmmaker who has made his peace with Europe to the point of dividing his time between homes in Ouaga and Paris is Idrissa Ouedraogo, a rising star of African cinema whose 1999 retrospective at the British Film Institute paid tribute to his "fierce determination to retain a poignant fidelity to the reality of the people, and his truly poetic rendering of the simplicity of the rural Burkinabe life." The director's first feature, *Yaaba*, won the International Critic's Prize at Cannes; his next, *Tilai*, took that festival's Special Jury Prize and won the Etalon at FESPACO, and his third, *Samba Traore*, was given the Silver Bear at Berlin.

A relaxed man with a kind of affable swagger about him, Idrissa, as everyone calls him, says he works out of Europe from simple necessity. "The gods don't love us here in Burkina; taking airplanes, making phone calls, everything is very difficult, very expensive," he says with a smile. "Here there are not so many opportunities to make films and to make contacts as in Europe."

Working in Europe, using non-African crews and non-African casts, has made Idrissa something of a controversial figure, an identity he easily shrugs off. "It is normal for people not to like me, because I can get financing outside of the traditional ways," he says. "All the people who speak about me, they can't do it. People speak about the imperialism of the American cinema. It is true, but there is a certain efficiency to American cinema that is a good thing, and we should try to have that as well."

More than anything, Idrissa wants his work to be seen not as African film but simply as film. "When I do some of these things, people say 'Stop, you are becoming white,' but I think cinema has no color. When I used French actors in one of my films, people wanted to kill me, they said, 'It is not African cinema.'

"But to me African cinema is a ghetto. When people think of African films, they want to see huts, they won't let Africans show something different. But Africa is not one country, it is a continent, and filmmakers are not alike, we are not the same. Even two American filmmakers do not have the same sensibility. Filmmaking is the personal thing you give to the world. You don't give your country or your continent, you give yourself."

While these issues get argued back and forth, the key underlying astonishment about FESPACO remains constant: how completely unlikely it is that this desperately poor country with a literacy rate of 18 percent, so underdeveloped that the UN's Human Development Report at one time ranked it 170th out of 173 countries, should have become the polished host of an event of this scale.

Some 80 to 90 percent of the Burkinabe toil as subsistence farmers, and one million others have moved to the neighboring Ivory Coast to find work. And, with life expectancy at forty-eight years, health is also a problem for residents, and for visitors as well. During the nineteenth century, West Africa was known as "the deadliest spot on earth," and even today buying medical evacuation insurance (it's not as expensive as it sounds) is strongly recommended for all tourists.

Prior to my own trip, having rashly requested what turned out to be dozens of pages of faxed warnings about malaria and other insect-borne maladies from our government's Center for Disease Control and Prevention, I became obsessed with health, even getting into arcane discussions with wilderness supply store clerks about the relative advantages of spraying or washing clothes with the powerful insect repellent Permethrin. Things got so bad that when I boarded my Air Afrique flight from Paris to Ouaga and saw an elderly man with a portable oxygen supply, my first thought was to wonder why I'd neglected to bring one myself.

In truth, when the festival began in 1969 as a small, informal Week of African Cinema showing but twenty-three films, no one expected it to grow into what it has. But, says Gaston Kaboré, who besides directing has for more than a decade been the secretary general of FEPACI, the Pan-African Federation of Filmmakers, "a conjunction of many desires, events and phenomena" gradually transformed what had begun as little more than a gathering of friends.

The first event was a 1970 conflict between the government of what was then Upper Volta and the French companies in charge of film distribution and exhibition, which resulted in an unprecedented state decision to nationalize those functions.

"It was a revolutionary thing, nobody thought that cinema could interest a government to such a point," remembers Kaboré, a vibrant, thoughtful man. "Many countries sent secret missions to know how we did this. The French retaliated by deciding not to furnish films, and we sent people to French-speaking places like Belgium and Algeria to buy them. It was like a little war.

"Eventually the French were obliged to reestablish the relationship, but those events gave us a kind of image in the world, that of a little country that, despite being one of the poorest, was the most interested in cinema and culture. So many things came from that."

The next event giving FESPACO a boost on the world film scene was a military coup in Upper Volta in 1983 that brought a thirty-four-year-old army captain named Thomas Sankara to power. A committed, innovative Marxist revolutionary, Sankara turned the country upside down, striking out against corruption and making childhood health and women's rights priorities. A charismatic populist, he sold off the government's fleet of official Mercedes, personally wrote a new national anthem, and changed the country's name to Burkina Faso, a combination of words in Moré and Dioula, the two dominant native languages, that together mean "land of honest, upright men."

Sankara saw the potential of FESPACO and embraced it wholeheartedly, and his reputation as a kind of African Che Guevara (he put slogans like "Fatherland or Death, We Shall Triumph," on everything from airport walls to tourist brochures) made attendance at the event attractive on a wider scale. His policies, however, alienated the country's traditional establishment (he for instance decreed that on one designated Saturday each month men had to do the family shopping) — and Sankara himself was overthrown and killed in another coup four years later, with his close friend and former corevolutionary Blaise Compaoré taking over as head of government, a position he still holds.

Though some African filmmakers have refused to return to FESPACO since Sankara's assassination, considering attendance a betrayal of the positive things he stood for, FEPACI's Kaboré has another point of view. Though "people from abroad thought Sankara created FESPACO, it was already established as a national concern when he came. He gave it a new impetus, brought a new vision, but cinema in Burkina does not belong to one government or one president. It is part of the patrimony of our country."

The phone rang promptly at 7 A.M. "The president will see you today," a cool voice said. "A car will pick you up outside your hotel at 10:30." They didn't have to tell me it would be a good idea to be ready on time.

Even before I left Los Angeles for FESPACO, the word had come from Burkina Faso that if I wanted an interview with Blaise Compaoré, "president of Faso, chief of state, president of the council of ministers," to give him his official title, it could be arranged. Since most film festivals won't even let you talk to the president of the jury, this was not an opportunity to be shrugged off.

In the years since he took control after that violent 1987 coup, Compaoré had gradually liberalized the political process, but when he ran for president in 1991, not surprisingly winning a seven-year term, the opposition parties boycotted the election, resulting in a voter turnout of only 25 percent. In 1998, he was once again returned to power.

Meeting me in the lobby of the Hotel Silmande was the owner of that cool voice, Naye Nell Diallo, a woman with a story that seemed straight out of a novel. Born in Alabama, she had worked for international organizations in Africa for ten years and then married one of President Compaoré's closest advisers, making her important enough to have been the first American ever to receive one of Burkina's highest national decorations, the Chevalier de l'Ordre National.

The president would be meeting us at his Camp David–style compound located about twenty minutes north of the capital at Zinaire, which means "that which has never been seen before" in Moré and is also the site of the village where Compaoré was born. "He relaxes here," Diallo explained. "In town, everybody tells him all the problems."

No signs, obviously, announced the compound, just a plain wire fence, a group of red and white painted concrete poles and a handful of lounging soldiers who casually approached our car. "I don't play with the military," Diallo said, rolling down the window and taking care to tell the soldiers who we were.

Surrounded by a large light brown wall over which green tile roofs were visible, the compound consisted of a main house and several smaller alcoves surrounding a swimming pool and a large open pavilion. The whole effect was tasteful but not opulent.

"This was donated to the president by his friends," Diallo said as we entered. "It will be eventually given to the country." Almost as an afterthought she added, "There is a lion around here somewhere, it was also given to the president," and sure enough, the unleashed animal could be seen pawing a nearby tree, with a handler hovering just behind. As we moved slowly toward the pool in the intense heat, the lion's presence made the entire situation seem only marginally more surreal.

Wearing black shoes, sharply creased black pants, and a white shirt worn outside, President Compaoré first played with the lion and then laughed when Diallo teased him that his staff says he's not the president when his shirt isn't tucked in. A handsome man with watchful eyes and a nice smile that he used only sparingly, the president gave serious answers to serious questions but relaxed more when the talk turned to film, revealing that thirteen years earlier he too had felt the restless urge to direct.

The result was a half-hour documentary on the National Commandos, a military group that he was then the leader of. "People consider them strange, like your Marines" he said in French, with Diallo translating. "So I made this to show they were real people." After he added that he has "many, many stories in his head for future films," Diallo suggested that he go to Hollywood and everyone laughed.

Asked if he'd seen many American films, the president smiled and, echoing the French cultural imperialism line, said, "Every film is American." It turned out he'd most recently screened, of all things, *Dirty Harry* with Clint Eastwood. The thought and the film seemed to amuse him. "It was in English, so I didn't understand everything, but it seemed a typical American film, with a lot of violence, a lot of action, and always a good car chase."

Asked if he'd seen anything from the current FESPACO, the president mentioned that *Guimba*, a film from neighboring Mali, had been brought out to the compound. "It's a good one," he said, which did not seem surprising, because, after all, who would want the responsibility of bringing out a film that was not good for the president to look at.

Guimba, in fact, was more than a good film, it was the popular winner of the Etalon de Yennenga that year, as well as many of the special jury prizes awarded by organizations as diverse as the European Union and Air Afrique. Directed by Cheick Oumar Sissoko, this gorgeously produced, bawdy costume drama about an evil sorcerer king, his mean-spirited, sexually active dwarf son, and the mother and daughter they want to force into marriage, mixes magic, spectacle, political commentary, and raunchy comedy in a vivid, spirited way. *Variety* later called it "in a class by itself among African films" and it achieved a rare level of American success for films from the continent, gaining a nationwide theatrical as well as a video release in the United States.

As for Burkina Faso, what with hosting FESPACO (with funding coming from the state and more than fifteen international partners) and being the headquarters for FEPACI, the country has gradually increased its commitment to film, even passing legislation providing for an admission tax on non-African films to help finance domestic production. One of Africa's few film schools is located in Ouaga, the city has dedicated a large, Claes Oldenburg–type public monument of a camera and reels of film to African filmmakers, and one of the main events of 1995's FESPACO was the opening of the continent's only climate-controlled film archive and library.

And FESPACO itself is hardly prepared to rest on its accomplishments. Feeling that "it is a pity that if a film is finished ten days after FESPACO it has to wait two years" for a festival showing, Secretary General Sawadogo talked about turning the event into an annual occurrence. "This would dynamize our industry, and as you say in the West, life is too short to wait to do something. The highway of information is coming, and we have to be present at some stops. Africa has 750,000,000 inhabitants, and we must give our own images to the world."

Havana

Scratch a Cuban, uncover a paradox.

To spend time in the crumbling but still heartbreakingly beautiful city of Havana, to talk to Cuban filmmakers during the Festival of New Latin American Cinema, is to hear the same words repeated over and over: contradictory, paradoxical, inexplicable, miraculous. "It's more difficult to explain what happens in Cuba in rational terms than to live here," says prominent director Gerardo Chijona. "If you're going to go by common sense, forget it."

To examine this small island's film history is to discover how far from conventional expectations everything is. Isolated and beleaguered by an American economic blockade that is almost as old as its revolution, Cuba should never have been able to muster the resources to develop any kind of film industry or to play host to a prestigious international festival dedicated to the socially conscious Latin American cinema.

Yet, starting in the late 1960s, when Tomás Gutiérrez Alea's *Memories of Underdevelopment* and Humberto Solás's *Lucia* impressed international audiences with their skill and brio, Cuba rapidly established itself as a world cinematic force.

And along with the industry the festival in Havana grew in the 1980s into the biggest, most important showcase for Latin American films, complete with Dionysian all-night parties that showcased the best in Cuban music. Helmut Newton shot the festival for *Vanity Fair*, Bob Rafelson slept in George Raft's celebrated circular bed at the Hotel Capri, Treat Williams flew in himself, Robert De Niro, and Christopher Walken in his private plane, and Cuban leader Fidel Castro took up so much of Jack Lemmon's time that the actor commented, "Anyone who can make me shut up for three hours has got to be extraordinary."

"During my years, cinema was born in the middle of the circus, the show was in the streets," says Pastor Vega, who ran the festival from its inception through 1990. "Everybody overseas thought that people were not happy here, that Cuba was a big jail. I decided to make a festival that was a film, theater, music, alcohol and sex festival, all together at the same time. In my opinion, that was cultural."

But all that was before what is known in Cuba as "the special period." Beginning in 1990 the tightening of the American blockade combined with the collapse of the Soviet bloc (which had accounted for 85 percent of Cuba's foreign trade as well as billions of dollars in foreign aid) to bring the island's economy to nearly a standstill.

The legalization of the American dollar as local currency in 1993 introduced a two-tier economic system to a society that had prided itself on its egalitarianism, making those without access to greenbacks feel like refugees in their own country and leading to too-true jokes with punch lines about bellboys making more money than brain surgeons. If Cuba had somehow managed to have a film industry and a festival before, surely this deepest of crises would bring everything to an end.

And Cuba's continuing economic miseries have made a difference in the relationship between its citizens and film. Estimates are that about half of Havana's movie theaters have been closed, victims of everything from persistent blackouts and weakened public transportation due to the lack of gasoline to projectors so ancient some are reportedly held together with string.

As a result, most Cuban moviegoing has transferred to television, especially a heavily watched Saturday night double bill that features hot items from Hollywood like *Forrest Gump* and *Jurassic Park*, all conveniently bootlegged off satellite transmissions. Enrique Colina, whose film analysis program on Cuban TV has lasted twenty-seven years ("I will ask for the Guinness record, especially if there is money," he laughs), says that "if relations with the U.S. become normal, it will be a big problem for the mass audience, because we couldn't afford to show these films."

The special period has also affected Cuba's prestigious Three Worlds International Film and Television School, where Francis Ford Coppola is fondly remembered for the day he cooked 4,000 gnocchi and fed the entire student body. Fernando Birri, the venerated Argentine director who was a founder of the New Latin American cinema movement and the school's first director, came back to celebrate his seventieth birthday. "Cuba is changing and the school will, too," he somberly told the students at a cake-cutting party. "The revolution is like a flame that seems about to be extinguished but stays alive. The flame is different, but it does not go out."

Yet, with all these problems, the paradoxical truth is that Havana's film festival is not only surviving but, helped by the country's ever-expanding tourist industry (more than 600,000 non-U.S. tourists spent an estimated $850 million in 1994), is actually prospering compared to where it was a few years ago.

Despite competition from festivals in Cartagena, Colombia, and Guadalajara, Mexico, Havana is still the major player in this market. The seventeenth competition in 1995 attracted more than ninety features from a dozen Latin American and Caribbean countries, with the top prize, the Gran Premio Coral, going to *Miracle Alley*, the highest-grossing Mexican film of the year and an Oscar candidate.

Of course, much has changed. "Now," says Gerardo Chijona, "we are making a festival according to our times." Which means, Pastor Vega unhappily notes, "no parties, only seminars, something 'serious,' in quotes." Almost everyone pays their own way these days, and the festival has begun to sell advertising space on everything from billboards to opening night tickets. Even Fidel Castro, far from schmoozing with Jack Lemmon, missed the event entirely. He was visible nightly on the TV news, however, visiting China and Vietnam, an exhausted presence in an overcoat being greeted by small children and giggling circus acrobats as he searched for tips on improving his country's economy.

As a concession to the Cuban population, the content of the festival has shifted markedly as well. Where in the 1980s the films shown were almost exclusively Latin American, now European, Asian, and even American films form a major presence. What audiences at more than twenty theaters in Havana and elsewhere in Cuba (the festival travels to half a dozen cities) may see has included *Pulp Fiction, Raise the Red Lantern, In the Name of the Father, Babette's Feast*, and dozens more. The reason: the country lacks the money to procure these films for regular theatrical runs, so if they were not brought in for the festival, Cuban audiences would not get to see them at all.

If all this sounds grim and somber, it shouldn't, because the passion and enthusiasm of the convivial Cuban population, the people the event is really intended for, make the Havana Festival just the opposite. Packs of lively fans crowd around the posted screening lists as if they were winning lottery numbers, and enormous throngs line up for hours in advance at major Havana theaters like the Yara and the Charlie Chaplin (the festival headquarters) and respond lustily to what's on screen.

It's difficult to think of another country where film is so important, has so transfixed an entire population from top to bottom. "Cubans," director Solás says flatly, "are the most cultured people in all Latin America." Moreover, adds veteran director Julio García Espinosa, "it's the only country in Latin America where people will stand in line to see Latin American films. Other audiences see that a film's in Spanish and they will not go."

Though Cuba was receptive to cinema even before 1959 (Solás remembers seeing such classics as *The Bicycle Thief* and *The Battleship Potemkin* by the time he was ten), there is no doubt that the Cuban Revolution raised the importance of film to a level never seen before. In

March 1959, less than three months after Castro's triumph, when other things were likely on his mind, the new regime's first cultural act was to create a state film organization, Instituto Cubano de Arte e Industria Cinematograficos, universally known by its initials as ICAIC.

Though propaganda and national self-image were reason enough to found ICAIC, Cuban filmmakers know, as critic Enrique Colina puts it, "all revolutions have family names, they depend on the people who make them." And if it wasn't for Alfredo Guevara, a courtly, cultured man usually seen with a sports jacket draped over his shoulders, the Cuban film industry might not exist at all.

Half a century ago, when Guevara was an undergraduate leader at Havana University, he took the advice of friends and sought out someone new on campus. "When I came back I said, and people remember my judgment, 'this student will either be the worst of gangsters or a new Jose Martí,'" the revered nineteenth-century Cuban patriotic leader.

The new student was Fidel Castro, and from then on Guevara's life intertwined passion for film and for the revolution. "I am who I am because Fidel is who he is," he says today. "If I hadn't met Fidel when I was so young, my path would have been different." Exiled in Mexico in the 1950s, he worked as a screenwriter and was Luis Buñuel's assistant on *Nazarin*. Always worshipful of Castro, he became one of the leader's most trusted assistants after the revolution, and he never forgot about film.

"Fidel knew I was obsessed with the idea of starting a film institute, we had talked about it a lot, but when I brought it up immediately after the revolution, he said, 'Don't think about that now,'" Guevara remembers. "But I think something was nagging at him, because a few months later he changed his mind and asked me to organize one."

Guevara became the first head of ICAIC, and his closeness to Castro immediately gave cinema considerable prestige. Also, since Guevara believed that ICAIC should be run by filmmakers and not bureaucrats, the institute gave Cuban writers and directors something unusual among state-run film systems: the ability to have give-and-take discussions about what can and cannot be filmed.

"Censorship is not organized in a bureaucratic sense, you have discussions and agreements," says Gutiérrez Alea, considered Cuba's master director both inside and outside the country. "In these thirty-five years that's the way it's been with me. No one has ever said, 'Do that.' I have made the films I wanted to make.

"When I went to Hollywood when *Strawberry and Chocolate* [which he codirected with Juan Carlos Tabio] was nominated for an Oscar, I said I would be happy to make films in America because they are seen everywhere, but I was afraid of the price I would have to pay. I am not sure I'd have the freedom I have in Cuba. That's the paradox."

Guevara eventually left ICAIC to be Cuba's delegate to UNESCO in Paris, but the crisis of the special period, which led to rumors that ICAIC would lose its independence and the film festival would go under, brought him back to run things again. "Fidel called me," Guevara reports, "and said, 'Come on, this is your problem,' and after all I am only a wink of Fidel." Coincidentally, Guevara also came back at a critical time for the philosophical direction of Cuban cinema. *Alice in Wondertown*, a satire on the Cuban leadership that won a Silver Bear at the Berlin Film Festival, was removed from local theaters after only four days of screenings, an unprecedented act that caused such a fuss that most Cuban filmmakers feel it helped pave the way for official toleration of the country's next controversial film, *Strawberry and Chocolate*.

While on the one hand, *Strawberry* is part of a Cuban tradition of irreverent comedies that mock the country's problems, it's difficult to overestimate the impact this film (Solás called it "extraordinarily audacious") had on Cubans, many of whom saw it numerous times despite long lines. Filled with inside references that only Cubans noticed, the picture not only treated homosexuality sympathetically for the first time, it also called passionately for tolerance of all differences of opinion. And it found a strong champion in Guevara, who even now speaks with feeling against the film's opponents, "those who think they are the most revolutionary but in fact are the most scared, the most conservative, the

Even all-business Cannes can look romantic in the right evening light. (Los Angeles Times photo by Al Seib)

John Malkovich deals with the media at a hectic Cannes press conference for Of Mice and Men. *(Photo by Patricia Williams)*

Few things symbolize Cannes as dramatically as beautiful women in gorgeous clothes: from left, actresses Claudia Schiffer, Andie MacDowell, and Gong Li get into the festival spirit. (Los Angeles Times photo by Al Seib)

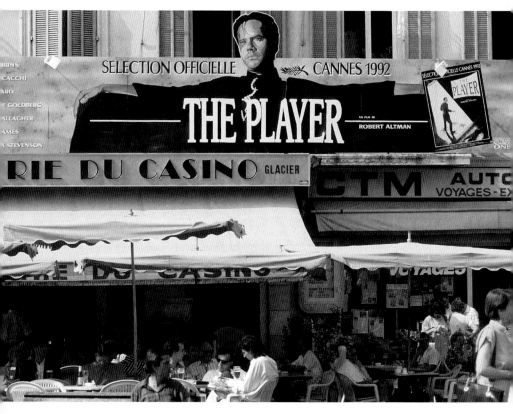

Tim Robbins as a Hollywood prince of darkness in The Player *hovers over Cannes's bustling street life. (Photo by Patricia Williams)*

Miramax's Harvey Weinstein, always a presence at Cannes, doing one of the things he does best: holding court with journalists after the press premiere screening of Dogma. *(Los Angeles Times photo by Robert Gauthier)*

For ten days every January, the vintage ski resort town of Park City, Utah, gets completely taken over by the Sundance Film Festival. Only careful planning prevents the twenty thousand film people who descend on it from swamping both residents and skiers. (Los Angeles Times photo by Al Seib)

Geoffrey Gilmore, director of the Sundance Film Festival, displays some of the hundreds of films submitted for entry in the prestigious independent event. The numbers of submissions in all categories display dramatic annual increases. (Los Angeles Times photo by Ken Hively)

Director Karyn Kusama,whose debut Girlfight *shared the Grand Jury Prize at the 2000 Sundance, strikes a typical Park City pose. (Los Angeles Times photo by Al Seib)*

Flyers for films at Sundance cover every available Park City surface, the movable as well as the stationary kind. (Los Angeles Times photo by Robert Gauthier)

*First-time film directors like Kaleo Quenzer of Memphis,
Tennessee, try all kinds of stratagems to get their films noticed
at Sundance. (Los Angeles Times photo by Al Seib)*

Postcard advertising FESPACO, the *Festival Panafricaine du Cinéma de Ouagadougou. The gigantic sculpture representing reels and lenses stands in Ouagadougou's Place des Cinéastes Africains and is dedicated to the filmmakers of Africa.*

Filippe Sawadogo, FESPACO*'s secretary general for more than a decade. On his desk sits the festival's top award, the Étalon de Yennega. (Photo courtesy of* FESPACO*)*

Burkina Faso stamp issued to honor the 100th anniversary of cinema as well as Gaston Kaboré, one of that country's top directors, and his film Rabi.

Burkina Faso stamp issued to honor the 100th anniversary of cinema and Idrissa Ouedraogo, another of the country's top directors, and his film Tilai.

Banner advertising the Sarajevo festival and the location of one of its newest theaters, part of the rebuilding of the city after the war. (Photo by Kenneth Turan)

A bombed-out theater in downtown Sarajevo. (Photo by Kenneth Turan)

The Sarajevo festival's 2,500-seat outdoor theater, located on a former school playground and squeezed between apartment buildings. (Photo by Kenneth Turan)

Mirsad Purivatra, director of the Sarajevo Film Festival, in front of a poster for The Perfect Circle, *the first film shot in the city after the 1995 cease-fire. (Photo by Kenneth Turan)*

Seen at the Midnight Sun Film Festival in Sodankyla, Finland: Surely the only thoroughfare within hailing distance of the North Pole to be named after a cult-favorite American director. (Photo by Kenneth Turan)

Finnish director Mika Kaurismäki, one of the founders of the Midnight Sun Film Festival, with the two official festival Cadillacs. (Photo by Kenneth Turan)

Sodankyla's Mouth of Lapland theater, the "Grand Palais" of the Midnight Sun Film Festival, located next door to a driving school. (Photo by Kenneth Turan)

Reindeer snacks at midnight and after are a Midnight Sun tradition. Some people never go to bed during the whole five-day festival. (Photo by Kenneth Turan)

Local acrobats entertaining moviegoers waiting for a screening to begin outside the Midnight Sun Festival's largest venue, an Italian circus tent that seats roughly five hundred. (Photo by Kenneth Turan)

A banner for Le Giornate del Cinema Muto, the festival of silent film, outside the venerable Cinema Verdi, in Pordenone in northeastern Italy. (Photo by Patricia Williams)

Four of the founders of the Pordenone event fool around with the Buster Keaton–inspired silhouette that is the festival logo. From left: Lorenzo Codelli, Piera Patat, Paolo Cherci Usai, and Livio Jacob. (Photo by Patricia Williams)

Pierce Lyden at eighty-eight: The bad guy in numerous B westerns relaxes where many of his films were made, the breathtaking Alabama Hills, three hours from Los Angeles, now home to the Lone Pine Film Festival. (Los Angeles Times photo by Don Kelsen)

An expectant crowd waits patiently inside the Telluride Festival's showplace theater, the restored 1914 Sheridan Opera House. (Photo by Patricia Williams)

people who think that the revolution rests on a single card and are afraid if it's moved the whole house of cards will collapse."

Despite *Strawberry*'s success, some Cuban filmmakers continue to worry about the future of films that combine pointed looks at contemporary reality with a popular, comedic touch. They notice that Gutiérrez Alea and Tabío's follow-up film, *Guantanamera*, a gleeful dark farce that follows a coffin from one end of Cuba to the other, did not open the festival as might be expected for such prestigious filmmakers (though it did end up winning the second-place Coral).

Also remarked on was that Rolando Diaz's *Melodrama*, a raucous and crowd-pleasing sex comedy with a noticeable social message, was absent from the official catalog and screened only once at a nonprestigious morning slot. Is subtle repression at work here, the exercise of personal taste by the powerful Guevara, or a combination of both? The answer depends on whom you ask.

For most Cuban filmmakers, however, the more pressing problem is getting films made at all. Economic problems have cut down Cuba's annual production from a dozen or more features to three or four, and coproduction agreements with other countries ("Now you have to convince a person who's living in San Tropez," Solás half-jokes) are close to essential before a project can proceed. "A film is a mobile factory, it needs fuel," says director García Espinosa, who ended up shooting his last film, *Reina y Rey*, across the street from his house.

Things are so grim, in fact, it is surprising to see any film production at all. "It's another miracle, because most Latin American countries, even though they're not facing our situation, are not producing any films," says García Espinosa, who ran ICAIC when Guevara was in France. Given the credit are a tradition of fighting windmills plus the goad of hard times. "Man grows when faced with difficulties," says Guevara, and Gerardo Chijona quotes Tolstoy to the effect that "art is born in chains and dies in freedom."

Even if films do continue to get made, a larger worry for thoughtful Cubans is what the materialism and opportunism the special period is breeding will do to the soul of the country in general and young filmmakers in particular.

Though he admits that "there is a danger that Cuba will become like Italy, the most cynical country in the world," director Solás believes otherwise. "The day in which the U.S.S.R. was dismantled was the happiest in my life, for though we had material splendor there was a lot of spiritual poorness. Now it is my hope that there will be a new Utopia here. We have been through so much, from the excesses of commercialism through wrongly done socialism, we don't want to come to the end of the century feeling shame."

Still, it is difficult finally to dismiss the thoughts of Solás's comrade, Gutiérrez Alea. Universally known by his nickname of Titon, the then-sixty-seven-year-old director talks with difficulty (he was to die of cancer a year later), but everything he says resonates with thought and feeling.

"The revolution was very clear in the beginning, but now it is another system," he says. "It didn't work one hundred percent, it didn't work a big percent, but those who didn't have to fight for this don't understand how important it is. Those of us who were inside want to save the moral values and dignity the revolution brought to this country, but it's not easy."

Gutiérrez Alea pauses and is reminded of a line from his 1968 *Memories*, when his protagonist says, "This island is a trap. We're too small and too poor. It's an expensive dignity." The director nods. "Yes, it's a very expensive dignity," he says. "But we have to try to pay for it, that's what I think. Because if you lose your dignity, you lose everything."

Sarajevo

Shell them till they're on the edge of madness.
— *Bosnian Serb commander Ratko Mladic,*
ordering the bombing of Sarajevo

The poverty of life without dreams is too horrible to imagine:
it is the kind of madness which is the worst.
— *poet Sylvia Plath, quoted in a press release*
from the Sarajevo Film Festival

SARAJEVO, BOSNIA-HERZEGOVINA — Many things come to mind when this city's name is mentioned, but a film festival is not one of them.

This was the city that survived the longest siege of modern history, more than forty-six months of exhausting, terrifying shelling and sniping from the surrounding Serb-controlled hills that damaged or destroyed 60 percent of its buildings. Approximately ten thousand died, 150,000 fled, and those that remained did without much of what we like to consider essential.

Often there was no communication with the outside world, no electricity, no power but foot power, and the city became ironically known as one big Stairmaster. There was no water for bathing or grooming, so people would show visitors photographs of how they looked before the war. There was no heat, so Aco Staka, the dean of Sarajevo film critics, a living encyclopedia of Yugoslav film who'd participated in festivals around the world, had to burn thirty-five years' worth of clippings to keep his family warm. And there was so little food during the siege that the average person lost close to twenty-five pounds.

In this formerly beleaguered location, once called "the world's biggest concentration camp" by a desperate Bosnian official, the notion of something as frivolous-sounding as a film festival, even nearly two years after the Dayton Accords was signed, seemed unlikely, anomalous, confusing. What was going on here?

While visits to more conventional festivals like Cannes or Sundance concentrate on rooting out what is new and different, the award-winners and trend-setters, Sarajevo promised a chance to examine the uses and purposes of film at ground zero, to get at the core of how the medium works and what it can mean to people no matter what their circumstances. Like the Hollywood director in Preston Sturges's classic 1941 *Sullivan's Travels* who takes to the road in an attempt to connect what he does with a larger reality, a visitor to Sarajevo could investigate the relevance of film in a setting considerably removed from the fleshpots of the studio system.

As Sullivan himself discovered, trips like this don't fit into tidy packages. On the one hand, film and the desire to see it turned out to be surprisingly central to the Sarajevo experience, not only in 1997 during the third year of the current festival — surely unique in its ability to offer a tour of the city's former front lines by the general who led their defense — but also during the worst days of the bombardment, when audiences literally put their lives at risk to go to the movies. "I was scared to death, running all the way with my cousin," said one woman about a clandestine expedition to see, of all things, *Basic Instinct*. "It was very dangerous, but we did it."

But the lesson of Sarajevo is more than the accurate but easy one that film can make the world whole. This is after all the Balkans, where nothing is straightforward and everything becomes politicized, where World

War I started after Gavrilo Princip, a Bosnian Serb seeking union with Serbia for his country, assassinated the heir to the Hapsburg throne. "You Americans are very lucky, you have a short history and a simple history," says filmmaker Srdjan Karanovic, the only Belgrade-based director to come to the Sarajevo Festival. "Here history is very complicated, there is conflict and remembrance from every period."

So while the Sarajevo Festival turned out to be a lively and exhilarating event, a miraculous breath of refreshing air experienced against overwhelming odds, film can only do so much in a city whose suffering has led to the removal of a Yugoslav monument to Princip (now seen as a Serb nationalist, not a liberator) and the wholesale changing of names of streets and buildings (the festival's headquarters hotel, once the Belgrade, is now the Bosnia) to fit new political realities. In front of the burnt-out shell of what was once Sarajevo's two-million-item library, deliberately targeted for destruction in an attempt to obliterate Bosnian culture, sits a plaque excoriating the "Serbian Criminals" responsible and ending with the stark peroration, "Do Not Forget. Remember and Warn!"

While the Sarajevo Festival in 1997 was noteworthy for films and filmmakers from Croatia, Slovenia, and Macedonia, three of Yugoslavia's former republics, no films came from Serbia. And the two movies from ex-Yugoslavia that have had the most impact on the world cinema scene, Emir Kusturica's Palme d'Or–winning *Underground* and Srdjan Dragojevic's festival hit *Pretty Village, Pretty Flame*, have not only not been widely seen here, they've been caught in a vortex of expectation-confounding survivor politics and generated anger and hostility that darkly oppose the acceptance they've received elsewhere.

Too much suffering and chaos has happened here for a tolerant, typically American, "let's forgive and forget" attitude to completely take hold, even among normally ecumenical filmmakers. More typical are the thoughts of director Ademir Kenovic, who stayed in Sarajevo during the war and whose *The Perfect Circle*, the first film shot in the city after the cease-fire, debuted at Cannes and opened the festival.

"I don't want to support in any way the stupid idea that what's needed is 'shake hands you filmmakers from Belgrade, you filmmakers from Zagreb, you filmmakers from Sarajevo,'" he said bluntly. "Nothing will be made better by that, by establishing again the feeling that everything is okay. It's not about us shaking hands, it's about war criminals going to the Hague."

Once, when Yugoslavia was a country that didn't need the word "former" in front of it, Sarajevo was a charming, sophisticated locale that elicited comparisons to Paris and San Francisco, somewhere visitors felt, it was said, "the air was freer." Located at a cultural crossroads, "Western for the East and Oriental for the West," it was also the kind of place, a resident of another Yugoslav city remembered, where you'd wake up hung over and happy but couldn't remember why you felt that way.

While elsewhere in Yugoslavia's six republics and two autonomous provinces people paid attention to whether their neighbors were Muslim, Roman Catholic, or Eastern Orthodox, Sarajevo was different. Nominally Muslim, by all accounts it was an anomaly, a hummingbird of a city that shouldn't have existed but did, the kind of genuinely multi-cultural metropolis often paid lip service to but not often achieved. A place with passionate film buffs like Dzeilana Pecanin.

A reporter during the war for *Oslobodjenje*, the city's resolute daily newspaper, who now works for the Voice of America's Bosnia Service in Washington, D.C., Pecanin confesses to being "completely hooked on the movies. Other girls were getting married, but I was in love with Robert De Niro and nobody else was good enough. When *Raging Bull* opened, me and a colleague took shifts queuing up for tickets on an incredibly long line so we could see it opening night. Everybody was ready to queue for hours, in the rain or the snow, for a movie."

Then came the war, chronicled in books whose titles form a litany of despair: *Balkan Tragedy, Origins of a Catastrophe, The Impossible Country, Slaughterhouse, A Tradition Betrayed, The Tenth Circle of Hell, Yugoslavia's Bloody Collapse, Yugoslavian Inferno, Yugoslavia Dismembered*, and dozens more. A war that made a special target of Sarajevo.

"My belief is that it was the place that most embodied tolerance and multiculturalism and that's why it had to be destroyed," says writer-director Phil Alden Robinson (*Field of Dreams, Sneakers*), who visited four times during the height of the war and wanted to return in early 1998 to shoot his script for *Age of Aquarius*, about an international relief worker who has a relationship with a woman from the city.

"Before the war it was the one place where people got along, a combination of small town openness and warmth and big city sophistication; it was the best vision we have of ourselves," Robinson explains. He in fact became so taken with Sarajevo during his visits that "I dream about being back there, and they're the happiest dreams. It's a city that intoxicates you for the right and to be honest possibly the wrong reasons: for what it is, for what it represents, for being the moral crisis of our time."

To visit Sarajevo nearly two years after the peace accord was signed in Dayton is to experience a city balanced on the push-pull of then and now. Remarkably recovered from the destruction it experienced but not yet free of memories of the past and a sense that the future is not secure, it is simultaneously exhilarating and depressing, depending on your point of view.

While almost all of Sarajevo's downtown has been rebuilt, pockets of the city are bombed out and desolate. The streets are surely safer than many in America, but landmines remain in the hills. Signs for Calvin Klein and an upcoming U-2 concert compete for space with announcements about de-mining. The much-shelled Holiday Inn, press headquarters during the war, looks completely new, but the high-rise building that housed *Oslobodjenje* remains a gaunt, ruined scarecrow. Stores carry everything from Yves Roche cosmetics to bananas from Ecuador, but the German deutschmark is the country's currency of choice, and credit cards, as one travel magazine put it, "are useful only for putting under the leg of a rickety table."

Still, Sarajevo remains what Mirsad Purivatra, head of the Obala Art Center and the film festival's director, calls "this crazy but charismatic town," inhabited by an unstoppably gregarious people who jam innumerable cafés and enthusiastically promenade through a pedestrian mall in the old town as if each night of pleasure has to make up for all those months of enforced misery.

Purivatra's nine-day festival (which announced 1997 attendance of 45,000, almost double 1996's total) is a key factor in that renewed spirit, so important to local morale that the Bosnian government has issued a stamp in its honor. It shows the event's modest centerpiece and main site for showing films, a year-old 2,500-seat open-air theater, artfully shoe-horned between buildings on an old school playground and complete with one of the biggest outdoor screens in Europe.

With financial backing from the city, UNICEF, the Soros Foundation, and private sponsors like fashion designer Agnes B., Renault, and Swissair, Purivatra and his programming director Philippe Bober put together a slate of sixty-five films from twenty-seven countries.

While many of these, well-traveled veterans of the festival circuit like *Guantanamera* from Cuba and Iran's *A Taste of Cherries*, were shown in the just-completed 200-seat indoor theater (also financed by international contributions), the spirit of the festival is most visible in its invariably sold-out outdoor screenings.

After French critics from *Le Monde* and elsewhere complained that the festival was becoming corrupted by Hollywood, the slate this time included European films as well as the first three features shot in Sarajevo: Kenovic's *The Perfect Circle* and Michael Winterbottom's *Welcome to Sarajevo*, both treated with deserved respect, and the unconvincing Spanish *Comanche Territory*, which was not. If audiences felt more than slightly surreal as they sat and watched wide-screen fictional representations of their former devastation, they were not about to let on.

Most of the open-air screenings, however, were of big-ticket block-busters like the *Jurassic Park* sequel, *The Lost World*, *The English Patient*, *Batman & Robin*, and *Con Air* (whose John Malkovich was the only major star to attend). These were a considerable treat in a city without a viable film distribution system whose remaining functional theaters were showing well-out-of-date films like Paul Newman in *Nobody's Fool* and

Demi Moore in *The Juror*. The energy of people jazzed to be at the movies marked these packed outdoor screenings, and the cheering was loud when Haris Siladjdzic, Bosnia's prime minister, announced on opening night, "This is a very great occasion for Sarajevo. Those that wanted to kill the spirit of Sarajevo did not succeed."

Even though, says critic Aco Staka, Sarajevo's initial importance in film was as an exotic Eastern locale for European directors, "cheaper than going to Baghdad," the medium was always important in Yugoslavia because it was important to Marshal Josip Tito, the country's ruler for more than thirty-five years.

When the annual Yugoslavian national film festival was held in an enormous Roman amphitheater in Pula (now in Croatia), Tito was often found on a nearby island, and boats would shuttle key films out to him every night. "When the boat returned with the films," remembers Goran Markovic, director of the delightful *Tito and Me*, "the projectionist would tell us 'he laughed' or 'he stopped the projection.' Very often the films he loved became favorites at the festival."

While Yugoslavian directors like Dusan Makavejev (*WR: Mysteries of the Organism*) and Aleksander Petrovic (*I Even Met Happy Gypsies*) became international favorites, being a filmmaker in a restrictive socialist country was not easy. After Sarajevo-based director Bato Cengic directed two films in the early 1970s that poked impish fun at the system, the delightfully sly *Life of Shock Workers* and *The Role of My Family in the World Revolution* (which features a cake in the shape of Stalin's head that the family avidly devours), he wasn't allowed to direct for ten years. Cengic eventually turned his BMW, one of the city's first, into a taxi to make a living. "I was a proscribed director," he says today with pride. "I was the example for all Yugoslavia."

Then came the war, and the shelling, and everything changed. Some directors, like Emir Kusturica, left the city. Others, like *The Perfect Circle*'s Ademir Kenovic, stayed to bear witness. He founded a group called Saga to document what was happening around him, "the absolutely different, horrible, outrageous, sometimes exquisite" things he saw, to record "the energy for life that was so strong it had to be documented." One of his projects, *Street under Siege*, a daily two-minute short about the inhabitants of the same block, ran for close to six months on the BBC and elsewhere around the world.

Because large movie theaters were obvious targets for shells and snipers and because electricity to run projectors couldn't be counted on, the only films seen during the war years were either on video or broadcast on television, both of which required loud, noisy portable generators to provide reliable power.

With bootleg cassette copies supplied by visiting journalists or international aid workers, Sarajevo TV stations would broadcast the same film dozens of times. Haris Pasovic, a successful theater director who recently completed the documentary *Greta Ferusic*, remembers, "It was not unusual to begin watching, have the electricity go off after fifteen minutes, and to continue in three months to watch again the same film. With *A Stranger among Us* (starring Melanie Griffith as an undercover policewoman in Brooklyn's Hasidic community), I needed three or four times over a year to complete the film."

"Sometimes you'd know a day in advance when it was the turn for your block to get electricity," says film buff Dzeilana Pecanin. "I'd go to the little video store by my house, and you can imagine, everything was outdated. I didn't mind, I'd take anything, especially if it was from before the war started. Watching it would completely take you back, you could completely escape from the horrors of reality for two hours."

Any kind of semi-organized public showings, however, took longer to get started, partly because, says Pasovic, "everyone felt 'this will stop next month.'" And, especially in the beginning of the war, Pecanin notes that "the shelling and sniping was so intense there was no way to go out, people hardly had the strength and courage to find food and water. All other, shall we say nice activities, completely died out."

Still, she says, "Many, many people, including myself, dreamed for nights and nights, we wished to see just once more another good movie. It was really hard, many people missed it as much as bread." Adds director Bato Cengic, who tried not to skip even one of 1997's festival screenings, "If I'm seeing five movies a day now, you can understand what a thirst I had during the war for movies. If I'd meet some friends and they'd seen a movie, I'd beg them to tell me every detail of what it was like."

After the war's first six months, says festival director Purivatra, "everyone was getting more and more crazy, and going out was the only way to survive. It was like being in jail but worse, because even in jail there are new faces with cruel stories that could be interesting to hear. In Sarajevo, no one was coming in, and you heard the same stories from neighbors so often it was very possible you were going to one day kill your neighbor. Everyone tried to make some kind of trip out of reality, and everyone wanted to be part of a group."

To answer these needs Purivatra and his wife Izeta Gradevic, who had founded Obala as a theater group in 1984, began in 1992 to sporadically hold word-of-mouth screenings of donated tapes in a dark and claustrophobic basement room accessible only through a bombed-out hole in a surrounding wall. (The wall now borders the festival's open-air theater, and that hole has been only partially repaired as an unobtrusive memorial to those days.)

"It was a war cinema, one hundred seats and a video beam projector, but in spite of the war, in spite of the shelling, it was packed every night we had a showing," Purivatra remembers. "The audience reception of films was completely different here. Sharon Stone naked in *Basic Instinct*, no big comment. But there was a dinner scene in the film that got two minutes of applause."

Also different, and a feeling that in some cases has not changed, was the reaction to violence on-screen. "After my war experience, I really can't get excited, not at all, by films like *Die Hard* or *The Rock*," says critic Aco Staka's son Vladimir, an *Oslobodjenje* reporter during the war who now lives in Canada.

"Those films are dead for me. People don't kill or get killed that way, it's not that pretty, not that iconographic."

As the only Serbian director to attend the Sarajevo Festival, Srdjan Karanovic was besieged by questions at his press conference. What was going on in Belgrade, everyone wanted to know, who was working and what were they up to?

Karanovic rattled off half-a-dozen films currently being shot, but he did not mention *Black Cat White Cat*, the latest work by Emir Kusturica, the former Yugoslavia's most celebrated director, a native and former resident of Sarajevo who now divides his time between Belgrade and France. Asked later why he left Kusturica off his list, Karanovic got off a "you must be kidding" look before answering, "I didn't want to disturb them. They hate him here; they treat him like a traitor."

Just a few years ago, such a response would have been unthinkable. Kusturica was Sarajevo's favorite son and a bona fide national cultural hero: when his Oscar-nominated *When Father Was Away on Business* won the Palme d'Or at Cannes in 1985, Yugoslavia declared a national holiday.

In fact, each of Kusturica's first four works won a prize at Europe's top three festivals, an unprecedented record that makes him one of the continent's most admired filmmakers. His debut, *Do You Remember Dolly Bell?*, won a Golden Lion at Venice in 1981, *Time of the Gypsies* won Best Director at Cannes, the Johnny Depp–starring *Arizona Dreams* took a special jury prize at Berlin, and *Underground* won him a rare second Palme d'Or at Cannes in 1995.

There was no Yugoslavian national holiday in 1995 because by then a viable Yugoslavia no longer existed. The country had split into five separate nations that were creating Europe's bloodiest nightmare since World War II. Kusturica's politics and his film, which dealt with the breakup, became the subject of intense debate and fury not only in Sarajevo and Belgrade but also across Europe. It led to the director's public decision to quit filmmaking (he's since changed his mind) and to turbulent, invariably hostile comments about him in his hometown. Probably nowhere in the world does the mention of a filmmaker's name elicit such an immediate and strong response from so many people as Kusturica's does here.

The reversal in this filmmaker's fortunes is a lesson in many things, from how deep the wounds of war can be to how puzzling yet intractable feelings of national identity and pride are and how central film has become to the expression of all of that. In fact, tell a film person from anywhere in the former Yugoslavia you have something complicated you want to discuss and before the questions can start, the reply comes, "It's about Kusturica, isn't it?"

Officially the country that still calls itself Yugoslavia (though it consists of only two of the former six republics, Serbia and Montenegro) is putting on a brave face. It regularly takes a booth in the international marketplace at Cannes and hands out a glossy booklet titled "Yugoslav Film: Culture of the Impossible." But to talk with directors from Belgrade, whether in person or on the phone, is to hear the voice of depression and despair.

They are as shocked as anyone, of course, at the carnage that has swept their country; "I never believed people could hate each other so much," says one director. "I never believed there could be hatred anywhere in the world like I've seen in this war." But even though they're aware that the world places the blame for the conflict almost unanimously on their country and on the ambitions of Yugoslavian president Slobodan Milosevic and Bosnian Serb leader Radovan Karadzic, it is impossible for most Serbs, who've viewed themselves as the downtrodden people in the region since they lost the battle of Kosovo Polje, the celebrated "Field of Black Birds," to the Turks in 1389, to see it the same way.

Even Karanovic, who says his presence in Sarajevo is testament to what he thinks, goes no further than "everyone is responsible, but the Serbian side is at least a bit more responsible." The causes were not religious or national, he says. "It was about robbery, as simple as that."

Echoing this is Srdjan Dragonjevic, director of *Pretty Village, Pretty Flame*, who says the conflict is "a new and primitive war for money, a kind of bloody capitalist revolution which established a new class of war rich."

Others, like *Tito and Me* director Goran Markovic, while bemoaning "this dirty war and this very big fascism in ex-Yugoslavia," see the conflict as a civil war (a claim that makes Sarajevans, who were attacked without provocation, apoplectic) and are troubled by Serbia's image in the world.

"It's not true that the whole Serbian nation are war criminals — you can't blame the whole nation for the people who made this war," Markovic says. "There were very, very brave people in Belgrade who were against this war. This simplification is very painful to me; I don't like this primitive view that Serbs are Indians, the Muslims are cowboys. It's a very complicated situation. You can believe me: even here we can't understand everything."

Sounding the most upbeat is *Pretty Village, Pretty Flame* director Dragojevic, but then again he is speaking from New York, where it's just been announced that he will codirect the upcoming *It's Me, the Hero* starring Harvey Keitel. This good fortune is the result of the worldwide reception of his film, which, though not immediately released in the United States, won awards at half-a-dozen festivals from São Paolo to Stockholm.

With scenes of Serbian soldiers looting and laying waste to Muslim villages, it was the first film to show Serbs in any kind of negative light and as such was a sensation in Belgrade and environs, with far and away the most admissions of any film of the year. "There were 5,000 people at the premier," reports Los Angeles–based actress Lisa Moncure, the only American in either the cast or the crew. "People were crying, there was something like a fifteen-minute standing ovation, it was an amazing experience for them to see the film. They were overwhelmed by it."

Given its willingness to show Serbs in a negative light, one might think that *Pretty Villages, Pretty Flames* would be embraced by Sarajevo, but that is not the case, and its reception illustrates the uncrossable barriers a war at home can create. The film has been exhibited in small private screenings, but its share-the-blame philosophy has attracted hostility rather than acclaim from a city that was the victim of a brutal siege and never had an aggressive thought.

"I think it's disgusting, a very nasty film," says director Haris Pasovic, head of the first Sarajevo film festival. "Saying that Serbia was so provoked it went too far in self-defense is a popular Serb theory, but it mixes everything up." Adds Mirsad Purivatra, who runs the current festival, "The idea that everyone is guilty on some level is unacceptable to me as a human being. Defending yourself versus killing to make a bigger country and destroying all traces of another nation's culture are not on the same level. That cannot be considered as everyone is guilty."

The situation with Emir Kusterica and *Underground* is, if anything, even more complicated, as is his film, which was initially called *Once There Was a Country*. An unruly, audacious, unashamedly excessive requiem for a dying Yugoslavia, it is an impassioned and surreal look at the past half century of that nation's history through the lens of a conniving opportunist who keeps a group of people prisoner in a Belgrade basement by convincing them that the war with the Nazis is still going on.

Underground impressed even those in the audience at Cannes who considered the film's tone over the top and its three-hour-and-twelve-minute length (since trimmed for domestic distribution) unnecessary. Equally impressive was Kusturica's passion for Yugoslavia. "I had to do something about a country that I loved. I had a need to answer the question, 'What happened?'" the director said of his reasons for making *Underground*. He also expressed displeasure, referring to Bosnia, at "now having to find myself under another flag, another country, another anthem," which is where things get complicated.

For while what's known as "Yugonostalgia" is a not uncommon feeling, promoting the preservation of Yugoslavia came to be viewed within Sarajevo as a justification for Serbian aggression. Kusturica's coupling that with what could at best be called diffidence toward Bosnia at a time when it was under merciless attack did not go over well back home.

In addition, many of the subtexts of *Underground*, like its blaming the country's current problems on the policies of Marshal Tito instead of Serbian self-aggrandizement, were often interpreted as legitimizing the war. The more Kusturica thought, possibly naively, possibly with calculation, that he was refusing to take sides, stepping outside of politics by distancing himself from the Muslim nationalist party that ruled Bosnia, the more his actions placed him in the Serb camp. And his having shot the film partly in Belgrade with a bit of Serbian financing did not help the situation.

All this contributed to nearly a year of bitter intellectual trench warfare about the film fought in the pages of French political journals. One side saw it as "a rock, postmodern, over-the-top, hip, Americanized version of the most driveling and lying Serbian propaganda." Then, as Adam Gopnik reported in the *New Yorker*, the other side responded that "the subject of the film wasn't nationalism at all, but the consequences of Communism — that it wasn't a national myth of Serbia but a transnational allegory of the post–Cold War period." That in turn caused celebrated Austrian novelist Peter Handke, in an essay published in this country as "A Journey to the Rivers: Justice for Serbia," to take yet a third tack and defend *Underground* precisely for its Serbian point of view.

Then, perhaps not surprisingly, in the middle of all of this Kusturica announced in the French newspaper *Libération* that he was quitting filmmaking. "I don't know to what extent this will relieve my enemies," he said, "but I do know that my friends will understand to what extent my life will be less burdensome."

Speaking from Belgrade, where he described his new film *Black Cat White Cat* as "something much lighter, a genre piece, pure comedy," Kusturica says his decision to quit filmmaking was as much a product of exhaustion as anything else. "Each frame is like a question of life and death for me," he said. "So in the middle of every movie I'm definitely deciding to stop."

Still troubling to him is the criticism he received for *Underground*. "I made a movie that was really the most sincere expression of how I felt about the past, that we were highly manipulated by politicians and the people who were leading us," he says. "I was doing all my best against propaganda and at the end I was accused of doing an Americanized version of Serbian propaganda. I felt in the middle of an Orwellian tragic comedy, I almost didn't find my way out of the 'Underground' story that was parallel to the *Underground* film."

Saying the reasons he left Sarajevo are "very personal," Kusturica is most troubled by the fact that his apartment (like the residences of many other people who left) has been confiscated by the state and given to a prominent writer. "In Sarajevo it's very profitable to scream slogans, to be against somebody who did not want to be involved so you can jump into his apartment and take all his belongings," he says. "Basically in the name of creating a multi-ethnic Bosnia they are looting our places."

To the people who remained in Sarajevo, it is the fact that Kusturica not only left but also did things like promote a Belgrade film festival while his birthplace was being bombed that caused the greatest anger against the director. "It's the 1940s—you don't give a concert with the Berlin Philharmonic. Everyone understands what is to be done when killers are killing people," says a furious filmmaker, and Dzeilana Pecanin, the film buff who moved to Washington, D.C., after the war, is even more direct. "I despise the person; I think he is the greatest jerk on earth. I don't care what he does, I don't think his movies deserve my eyes."

As to why Kusturica made the choices he did, there are as many opinions as people happy to offer them, though, given the suffering and death in the city, the willingness to give the director the benefit of any doubt is nonexistent. He's reviled as careerist, narcissistic, and vain, and, ironically given his insistence that he wanted to be outside of propaganda, his involvement in politics is cited by almost everyone as a cause of his plummeting esteem.

"Politics is fatal for cinema," says Aco Staka, the dean of Yugoslavian critics, speaking the words in English to accent their importance. Staka's son, former Sarajevo journalist Vladimir Staka, agrees but sees things in a wider perspective.

"The main reason is that people felt abandoned by him. He was the principal bearer of the Sarajevo spirit and he switched," the younger Staka says. "If there was a lot of irrational reaction against him, one should understand the irrational situation we were in. During the war people identified with the government that was struggling to keep as many people alive as possible, and he gave numerous statements that were critical of the regime. If you're an artist, you'll do anything, you'll sell your soul to the devil to get money to make movies. And now he bears a terrible mortgage in Sarajevo."

To Americans, who create the world's most popular films but look on the medium as a weekend diversion that can easily be done without, Sarajevo's kind of intense, almost heart-rending passion for film has to be unexpected, almost disconcerting. Some of it, Sarajevo residents say, is simply a heightened version of the love of film as (in Mirsad Purivatra's words) "the most alive medium in the world today" that cineastes everywhere share. But when you come to probe film's meaning in a city under siege, you hear different notions, expected ones like the need to escape and some that tend to go unspoken and unreflected on elsewhere.

Mentioned frequently was fear of cultural isolation, a determination not to be alone in the world. "Hunger is not the worst thing that can happen to a person," says director Bato Cengic. "As for death, I was ignoring it. If grenades went off, I didn't turn around. I was superior compared to death. But what made me unhappy and sad was that I didn't have communication with the civilized world. That was the worst part." Adds Dzeilana Pecanin, "In spite of all the hardships we never gave up on the things that made us human beings, not animals."

Linked with that was the way going to the movies was an act of defiance, a proof, says critic Staka, that the city and its residents were unapologetically alive. Seeing films also helped provide what was most denied Sarajevo's citizens, an ordinary feeling unnoticed during peacetime, the sense of simply being normal.

"You don't have to have everything fine to want to see movies," says

Haris Pasovic. "You see them because you want to connect, to communicate from your position on the other side of the moon, to check whether you still belong to the same reality as the rest of the world. The favorite question of journalists during my festival was 'Why a film festival during the war?' My answer was 'Why the war during a film festival?' It was the siege that was unusual, not the festival. It was like we didn't have a life before, like our natural state of mind and body was war."

Held for ten days in October 1993, in the teeth of the siege and the shelling, the Pasovic-run one-time-only Sarajevo International Film Festival symbolized the furious and foolhardy daring of those determined to watch films. Vladimir Staka remembers it as "crazy, something like a 'Mad Max' situation. People were shot and died on the way to the festival." It was also an event that completely embarrassed the UN, which found itself refusing, possibly on orders from the British government, to fly stars Vanessa Redgrave, Jeremy Irons, and Daniel Day Lewis into the city for the event. "So we had our scandal," says Pasovic ironically, "just like every big film festival."

Getting the films themselves in proved equally difficult, and the festival likely never would have happened if not for Mexican director Dana Rotbart, now the wife and then the companion of *Perfect Circle* director Ademir Kenovic.

"Since I had a Mexican passport and could get in and out of the siege, Haris asked if I could help him," she says. "I couldn't telephone from Sarajevo because we had access to a satellite phone for only five minutes every fifteen days. So I sent faxes to everyone I'd met in a year of traveling with my film. Then I took a plane to Paris and for a week or ten days called every possible person I knew or didn't know. It was totally nonprofessional, there were no contracts, I just was getting tapes, tapes, tapes."

Rotbart ended up with 170 cassettes, including documentaries, shorts, and cartoons, enough to fill seven large well-packed boxes weighing in the neighborhood of 150 pounds. Which presented a problem, for the regulations on the UN military flight she had to take back allowed only 22 pounds of baggage per person.

"The soldier at the airport was very difficult. He told me the only way I was going to get those tapes on the plane was if I carried all the boxes myself in one trip. I put ropes on the boxes. It was extremely heavy, heavy, heavy, but I concentrated very hard and dragged them to the plane, where I made an impolite sign to the UN soldier." There was, however, a price to be paid. "I broke my back, literally, I dislocated two discs and I still can't pick up anything heavy." A small smile. "Maybe I should sue the UN and really get rich."

What started with Pasovic's determination "to see some new films" ended up with a staff of eighty. "We arranged with a tobacco factory to give us cigarettes, and a bakery donated extra flour and cooking oil, and everyone was paid with that," Pasovic remembers. Tickets were given away, more to control crowds than anything else, and when they appeared for sale on the black market, Pasovic knew the event would be a success. There was criticism about logistics, and even the director admits that wartime conditions meant the festival was "a bit chaotic, not always very well organized," with schedules so jumbled it was often impossible to know what was playing when. Still, Dzeilana Pecanin remembers crowds in front of theaters on opening day, "so excited and happy, just mesmerized by the chance to go into a real movie theater that nobody thought, 'I am standing right now in a street where any minute the Serbs can throw a shell and that's it.'"

Which is in fact what happened the second day. "The shelling was so intense and so strong it was too much," says Pecanin. "Absolutely I'm sure the Serbs knew how unhappy it made us. They just wanted to destroy any sign of humanity, any chance of us feeling like decent civilized human beings. I had a ticket to see Francis Ford Coppola's *Dracula*, and how strongly I can remember the feeling of pain in my chest. It was almost physical. I don't think I ever hated them so much."

Seeing films is not so difficult now, but the current festival, begun by Purivatra and Obala two years after Pasovic's event, remains essential for the city's residents. Because they felt abandoned and disowned by the West during the war, says Vladimir Staka, "the main drive that people have is to feel that they are part of the scene," to reconnect with the culture of the larger world.

"They believed they were part of Europe, and they paid a terrible price for that perception," says director Phil Alden Robinson. "They're very angry that Europe does not embrace them; they still don't understand why we don't get it." The way the city's desire not be forgotten coincides with the West's guilt at having forgotten for as long as it did is the dynamic that makes the festival possible.

Allied to this ambition to regain the cosmopolitan status that film is the most direct route to, the festival's presence also speaks to deeper needs that most Sarajevans do not necessarily talk about. For nothing infuriates residents of this city more than the perception that, to paraphrase *Chinatown*, "It's the Balkans, Jake," that this is a place apart, a locale so riven by ancient hatreds as to be beyond saving.

For people here are intensely aware, as historian Maria Todorova has written in *Imagining the Balkans*, that that nominally geographic term has become "one of the most powerful pejorative designations in history, international relations, political science, and, nowadays, general intellectual discourse." To host a film festival, that preeminent symbol of the cross-pollination of modern culture, is a way of removing the stigma of the bloody Balkans, a way of reminding the world that this city fought a war because it believed it had earned a place in that cosmopolitan artistic cosmos.

In truth, the most powerful feeling generated by being in Sarajevo and attending the festival is the chilling one that if the apocalypse could visit a sophisticated city like this, it could happen anywhere. Almost as an aside, a Belgian director at the festival noted that film crews from the two ethnic halves of his country, the Flemish and the French, are never mixed, and he caused an uproar at home when he did so. Adds Phil Alden Robinson, "A Sarajevan asked me to imagine that the Ku Klux Klan completely controlled our government and media for two years and sent out nothing but racist propaganda. Couldn't we have a race war in our country after that?" So if you choose to weep for the Balkans, it shouldn't be because they're unique, but because they're not.

Given how much Sarajevo has gone through to get to where it is, it would be unfair to leave on a pessimistic note, and, fortunately, it's not necessary to do so. Because a major part of 1997's festival was an extensive three-times-daily series of children's matinees of films like *The Lion King*, *The Little Princess*, and *Pocahontas*, which started when director Purivatra realized that the four-year siege meant that a generation of children hadn't had the opportunity to see movies on a big screen.

Held in conjunction with local schools, which bused the students to the thousand-seat Bosnian Cultural Center, these matinees were joyous and uplifting, a merry maelstrom of wall-to-wall children whose enthusiasm for the medium and for simply being alive went straight to the heart.

To see these small survivors, children who learned to sleep through shelling but were terrified when reconnected telephones started to ring after the war, literally bounce up and down in the purity of their anticipation and glee turned out to be as much of a privilege as this city provides. To witness the power of the unadulterated enjoyment film can provide, to experience the resilience of children, is to believe Sarajevo's permanent renewal is possible after all.

Midnight Sun

Finland is a law unto itself.
— *Peter Cowie, Finnish Cinema*

SODANKYLA, FINLAND — It's midnight not in Savannah's celebrated Garden of Good and Evil but in this distant Lapland village a hundred miles north of the Arctic Circle, a remote, mosquito-plagued time and place that, all things considered, might be even stranger.

It's not just the startling presence next to the town's high school of a genuine circus tent, vivid blue with yellow and red stripes and big enough to make the performers of Fellini's *La Strada* envious. A tent out of which into the breezy midnight air float the unmistakable tones of Ian McKellen's cultivated author in *Love and Death on Long Island* insisting to Jason Priestley's Hollywood hunk, "If Shakespeare were alive today he'd be doing something like *Hot Pants College.*"

And it's not just the crowds fighting off swarms of mosquitoes celebrated enough to be on picture postcards ("It's Finland's national bird," someone says) while they line up for freshly cooked reindeer sausage on a street whose name you have to look at twice to believe: "Samuel Fullerin katu," surely the only thoroughfare within hailing distance of the North Pole to be named for a cult-favorite American director.

No, what makes all this especially strange is that even though clocks are striking midnight, a bright and cheerful sun is shining everywhere. Sun on the sign, on the circus tent, sun warming the wonderful Zen-like spareness of Sodankyla's wooden Lutheran church, built in 1689 and one of the oldest in the country, sun illuminating the large, muscular statue of a Lapp herder wrestling a reindeer, which sits on the town square. For this is one of those celebrated Scandinavian white nights, when, as the tourist brochures never tire of testifying, "the sun never slips below the horizon and a day lasts more than two months." If a celebration of cinema were to locate itself here and now, it could hardly be everyday, and no one has ever confused the Midnight Sun Film Festival with anything close to ordinary.

Held each year in mid-June (theoretically a week before the mosquito season starts, but, the local joke goes, the mosquitoes aren't always informed), this the world's most northerly film festival has also been called "the world's most impractical location," "one of the weirdest events in the film world," and, in its own literature, "something you have never even dreamt about . . . five days and nights during which life is far from being wasted with trivialities . . . the most informal and craziest festival in the world."

Despite, or perhaps because of all this, the Midnight Sun Festival, which recently celebrated its fourteenth year, has established quite an international reputation. In a world of carbon copy festivals, this event is unduplicatable, one of a kind, creating its own particular ambiance and spirit as it encourages its participants to get high on a quintessentially Finnish combination of cinema, summer sunlight, and, yes, strong spirits.

Though it has its share of new films, the Midnight Sun is better known for in-person tributes to some of the most celebrated and eclectic names in the history of film, including Michael Powell, Jacques Demy, Monte Hellman, Krzysztof Kieslowski, André de Toth, Roger Corman, Claude Chabrol, Stanley Donen, John Sayles, Terry Gilliam, and Wim Wenders. Its relaxed charms caused one British critic to call it "the world's best film festival," and another, in a claim the Finns liked even better, insisted it was in fact "the second-best festival in the world."

The Finns favor that description because it fits with the easygoing, unruffled quality that the festival, which thinks of itself as "the anti-Cannes," takes pride in. Fiercely casual, with not a single necktie visible anywhere in town, the Midnight Sun Festival doesn't so much encourage as insist on low-key naturalness. "Our holy principle," says Peter von Bagh, Finland's best-known film writer and the festival's director, "is never to have any formalities."

Also, the Finns well know that as far as the rest of the world is concerned this is an unlikely country (not to mention neighborhood) for a major festival. Guidebooks tend to call Finland "Scandinavia's most culturally isolated and least understood country" and its language, part of the notorious Finno-Ugric family, "one of the world's strangest and most difficult." The country's population is small (5.1 million all in, with density in Lapland a spread-out five per square mile) and homogenous: non-Lutherans equal only 14 percent of the total and non-Finns make up a bit more than 1 percent of the 5.1 million, the lowest percentage in Europe.

And Finland's film culture, despite giving actionmeister Renny Harlin (*Die Hard 2, Cliffhanger, Deep Blue Sea*) to Hollywood, is one of the world's least celebrated. The British Film Institute's 1975 *Cinema in Finland*, the first English-language study of the subject, lamented "the aesthetic poverty of traditional Finnish cinema," and Peter Cowie's *Finnish Cinema* admitted that "for decades the cinema has been the ugly duckling of the arts in Finland." And this from the country's nominal champions.

The saving grace in all this is that, despite their reputation for Calvin Coolidge–type parsimoniousness with words, the Finns have a terrific albeit deadpan sense of humor. Take this gloss on early history from an official government tourist brochure: "When the ice went away the Finns arrived, and from that time until the 14th century they got by as best they could on a diet of clan warfare." Or this thought in a brochure about a new festival in Savonlinna in eastern Finland: "Had it been possible in the 16th century, Erik Axelsson Tott would have started a film festival in Savonlinna. The setting would have been perfect but, unfortunately, the times were not."

There is a similar droll quality to the Midnight Sun, a playful dada "let's do a festival in the middle of nowhere" spirit, says Mika Kaurismäki, one of the event's founders along with his brother Aki. In fact, Mika adds, just possibly seriously, "the original idea was to do a counterfestival in January, when it's dark all the time, to have open-air screenings in the freezing cold with films projected on screens made of snow." Maybe next year. . . .

To understand the Midnight Sun Festival, it helps to understand the Kaurismäki brothers, film directors both, who have jointly given Finland its most prominent place ever in the international film community. Though a smattering of Finnish films had achieved outside recognition over the years — *The White Reindeer* and *The Unknown Soldier* in the 1950s, *The Earth Is a Sinful Song* in the 1970s — the Kaurismäkis, especially younger brother Aki, one of the youngest filmmakers to have a Museum of Modern Art retrospective, raised the bar considerably.

Aki's *Drifting Clouds* was in the official competition at Cannes in 1996, and his silent *Juha* debuted at the New York Film Festival. Between them, the brothers have brought their striking blankly comic fusion of personal and Finnish sensibilities (including extensive use of the popular wacked-out rock band with foot-long pompadours, the Leningrad Cowboys) to both the Midnight Sun Festival and films that have played in something like sixty-five countries worldwide.

The brothers no longer live full-time in Helsinki (Aki has a home in Portugal, Mika in Rio), but they are still very much admired, and the way they've in a sense institutionalized the Finnish sense of humor has made them a presence either physical or spiritual at almost every festival. The night before 1999's event, it was Mika who organized a Helsinki treat for overseas guests, ferrying them to a dinner in the official festival cars, which, in a typical Kaurismäki touch, turn out to be vintage mint-condition Cadillacs, a black 1959 and a candy-apple red 1961.

The night ended at the brothers' one-of-a-kind Helsinki entertainment complex. This includes a coffee house, a pool hall decorated with stills from *The Hustler,* and a gorgeous two-screen art house called the Andorra, named after the tiny European country the brothers were once half-seriously thinking of emigrating to, and distinguished by a classic scene from Sergei Eisenstein's *Ivan the Terrible* reproduced not in marble but in cut linoleum on the lobby floor.

Right next door is another puckish Kaurismäki enterprise, the Moscow Bar. Determined, Mika insists, to be unpopular, the brothers (who have a production company called Sputnik) named the place in memory of "the totally unfashionable Soviet Union" and chose to feature what the USSR was known for, "expensive drinks and bad service." The Moscow, nevertheless, is always crowded. Maybe it's the hand-lettered sign behind the bar that reads, "In Lenin We Trust, Others Pay Cash." Or a photocopy on the wall of the actual Finnish declaration of independence from Mother Russia, signed in 1917 by Lenin, Stalin, and Trotsky and, with a flourish at a slightly later date, by Aki Kaurismäki.

It is possible, for those in a leisurely frame of mind, to take a special "festival train" from Helsinki to Lapland, a multi-hour trip that once featured pictures projected in 35 mm, advertised as "the world's only cinema on rails on the trains!" But a dispute with the state railway has temporarily derailed the movie projection, and I chose instead to join a group flying into Rovaniemi, a city right on the Arctic Circle with a street plan, suggested by celebrated Finnish architect Alvar Aalto, patterned after a pair of reindeer antlers. Rovaniemi is also the home of a thriving tourist attraction called Santa Claus Village, whose 700,000 letters received per annum encourages one Finnish guidebook to call it "the true home of Santa Claus, no matter what the Swedes or Norwegians may say."

Finland, the home of Nokia mobile phones, is considered the most wired nation on earth. From the air, however, with reindeer sausage sandwiches for the in-flight snack washed down by strong Lapin Kulta beer, the country presents a different face: many but by no means all of its 187,888 lakes are visible, and trees are remarkably thick on the land. Forests are in fact said to cover three-quarters of the country's surface, giving the vistas a dense, verdant, almost pagan feeling.

Viewed from the ground, Lapland, the northern third of Finland, is a green and empty land, but a place whose clear air and great sense of space allows the spirit room to expand. A festival bus takes us the hundred miles to Sodankyla, a trip noticeable for its almost complete lack of cars and advertising signs: with hardly anyone on the roads, there's no one to try and sell to.

An overgrown town of some 11,000, Sodankyla, like most of Lapland, had to be rebuilt after World War II, when the retreating Germans torched just about everything, leading to mordant local jokes like "Vacation in Finland: Bring Matches." One of the things that was rebuilt was the movie house, located next to a driving school and called the Lapinsuu Teattrerissa, the Mouth of Lapland Theater. It's said to be the only such theater in all Lapland (Mika, in a joking reference to Cannes, calls it the "Grand Palais"), a key factor in the decision to locate the festival here. Inside its lobby it's the 1950s all over again, as vintage color-tinted photos of MGM stars like Clark Gable, Ava Gardner, Stewart Granger, and Elizabeth Taylor line the walls, unmoved for decades.

Screenings at the Midnight Sun also take place in two other venues, the local high school's gymnasium (with the basketball backboards neatly folded against the wall) and that enormous circus tent next door, purchased by the Kaurismäkis from Italy for the event's first year. Unlike the screens at most festivals, the three venues keep going close to twenty-four hours a day, with a sign at the box offices reminding the unwary that "the festival day changes at 9 A.M." In other words, films that start at 3:45, 5:45, and 8:30 on a Saturday morning are listed at the end of Friday's schedule. For no one's crazy enough to actually get up for these screenings; the sane thing to do, at least up here, is not to go to sleep in the first place.

Given that you can't show movies without darkness, the festival organizers are pleased with the genial conundrum of being in a locale where the only place you can experience darkness is inside a movie theater. "It gives us our flavor," says Mika Kaurismäki, with fest director Peter von Bagh adding, "This dialogue with darkness and light is our very special circumstance, part of the subconscious effect of the festival."

Experiencing the white nights of the midnight sun was the key reason I'd wanted to visit this festival, but I'd recently seen *Insomnia*, an excellent Norwegian thriller directed by Erik Skjoldbjaerg and advertised as "introducing film blanc (film noir from the land of the midnight sun)," an experience that made me wonder if I'd made the right choice.

Insomnia stars Stellan Skårsgard as a Swedish detective investigating the murder of a seventeen-year-old high school student in Norwegian Lapland. One of his main obstacles turns out to be the pitiless twenty-four-hour sun, a terrifying, disorienting, invasive light that he can't seem to prevent from seeping into his room and destroying all possibility of sleep. The implacable light tortures and torments him with its unnatural perverseness, and there are moments when he all but collapses under its relentless pressure. What if all this happened to me? Would I start confessing to imaginary crimes, or even to real ones?

Fortunately, the midnight sun turned out to be not only benign in its effects but, with a knack for putting everyone in a festive mood, also quite wonderful to experience. A sun that never sets is frankly exhilarating and made me feel light-headed and giddy, in permanent high spirits. Nominally adult, I felt increasingly like a child who's getting away with something, who can't believe he's lucked into an unexpected, never-ending recess.

This isn't to say that the whole thing isn't formidably disorienting. It's not so much that you can't tell the difference between day and night, it's that you can't figure out why you should care, can't decide whether, except to deal with movie starting times, there's any point in ever looking at your watch. The situation is especially unsettling when you come out of a theater at 2 A.M. into that cheerful warm light and have such an instinctive expectation of darkness you feel as if you're expecting a stair that's no longer there.

What you don't feel like at all is sleeping. Though my room at the Scandinavian modern Hotel Sodankyla came with heavy curtains capable of blocking out even extra-strength sun, I was reluctant to give up on the light. I walked up and down Sodankyla's single main street, pretending to be Jussi Björling singing the great tenor aria "Nessun dorma" ("no one sleeps") from Puccini's *Turandot*, and, periodically forgetting what time it actually was, wondered why all the stores were closed. As opposed to sixteenth-century Europeans, who rioted when Pope Gregory's calendar reform robbed them of what they felt were ten days of their existence, I felt my lifespan was being added to, that to sleep would have been to squander a gift literally from the gods.

Most year-round residents of Lapland feel the same way. For them, the summer is a window of opportunity to live more fully, to sit in the sun eating ice cream (a national warm-weather mania) and feeling thunderstruck at all that light. It's also a time, because everyone feels in a celebratory mood, to do very little sleeping and a good deal of drinking.

While people here are already famous for take partying seriously ("Why Do the Finns Drink So Much?" is a chapter in one guidebook, and an estimated 10 percent of government revenue comes from the sale of alcohol at state-run Alko stores), the midnight sun accentuates the trend. Drinking is endemic but surprisingly low key; it's hard to think of another film festival where the people who run it pass around pre-screening pints of Kosken Korvan, the extra-strong Finnish vodka that's been called "ideal for assessing the strength of your stomach lining." Try it, they say as they hand over the bottle, you'll like it, and, surprisingly enough, you do.

It's not only foreigners who are stunned by Lapland's endless light. The festival, which racks up close to 20,000 admissions, is attended almost exclusively by Finns from all over the country (last year two young girls from rural France arrived and caused a sensation), and they, too, have often never seen the true midnight sun. Olli Saarinen, for example, and his girlfriend Leena Tikkanen hitchhiked and drove ten hours from Imatra in eastern Finland to get here. "Is this something you can see in Hollywood?" Olli asked her as they motored down the sunny main street in the wee hours of the morning. "It's really weird," Leena reported the next day. "I was really tired and waiting for the sun to go down so I could go to sleep, but the sun didn't go down at all."

Mostly young, mostly traveling with backpacks almost as tall as they are, the fans who call themselves "filmihullu," film mad, are the pride of the festival. They buy a twelve-admission card (which costs about $50) because, says Kristina Haataja, the festival's unflappable program manager, "if they feel, 'Okay, maybe I'll see one or two films,' they won't come in the first place."

Since Sodankyla has only two small hotels, most of the Midnight Sun audience — protected by omnipresent canisters of locally manufactured Johnson Off! mosquito repellent that look way too toxic for sale in the United States — spills over into several campgrounds in the area. With the movie theater and the high school offering some of the only public darkness for miles around, sleeping in your seat is a frequently taken option, as is dozing off curled up in your sleeping bag under the big blue circus tent. "When Paul Schrader showed his *Cat People* in the tent," recalls Mika Kourismaki, "he had what he called an ultimate festival experience: watching his film one morning with some people in sleeping bags making love on the ground."

Because this is a country that has only roughly 350 movie screens, one of the lures of the Midnight Sun Festival for Finnish audiences is the rare chance to see new foreign-language films in the eclectic "Pearls of New Cinema" section, which has included such diverse items as Erick Zonca's *The Dreamlife of Angels*, Shohei Imamura's *The Eel*, Bernardo Bertolucci's *Besieged*, and Hal Hartley's *Henry Fool*.

Often, these directors have come to Sodankyla with their films and have been inspired by the locale to do work of their own. Spain's Juan Carlos Medem thought up *Lovers of the Arctic Circle* after a Midnight Sun visit, and Mexican director Gabriel Retes, here with his wife and collaborator Lourdes Elizarrarás showing his deft and surprising comedy

Welcome, promised to make a film about an understandably frustrated midnight sun vampire.

Paradoxically, says program manager Haataja, because theaters in many Finnish cities "only show a few American big things," one reason Finns come to Sodankyla is to see the year's best of their own films. Nineteen ninety-nine boasted an unusually strong showing for home-made movies at local box offices ("Cool Finns — hot tickets," headlined *Moving Pictures*), and the Midnight Sun made a point of showing the country's top film, Olli Saarela's *Ambush*, which turned out to be an enjoyable, self-consciously heroic epic about a handsome young lieutenant and his platoon fighting behind enemy lines in the struggle against Russia at the end of World War II called the Continuation War. Imagine a Finnish *Saving Private Ryan*, and you'll be surprisingly close.

The Midnight Sun also provided a chance to see the loopy Finnish production that is the festival's signature film, a broad 1951 farce called *Rovaniemi Marketplace* whose cast was featured on the artwork for the first Midnight Sun Festival and has appeared on many of the posters since.

With accordion music by the locally beloved Esa Pakarinen punctuating the story of the Lapland misadventures — there really isn't a more appropriate word — of three bumpkins prospecting for gold, *Rovaniemi Marketplace* proved to be (at an 8:15 A.M. screening with its share of people sleeping and/or amiably sharing alcohol) one of those easy-going light comedies that's perfectly understandable without the assistance of subtitles.

According to the festival's program notes, this was "the first Finnish film where the heroes were ordinary poor wanderers, vagabonds and rascals, who later in the 50s dominated our film industry." "These comedies were part of our childhood, our Finnish heritage and tradition," says Mika Kaurismäki, while Peter von Bagh adds, with typical dryness, "It's a sacred film for me, but I'm a man of bad taste."

The one thing that can be said with assurance about *Rovaniemi Marketplace* is that it wouldn't get a similar place of pride at old-line events like Cannes, and it was a troubled frustration with that festival and others like it that led directly to the creation of the Midnight Sun Festival.

"As young filmmakers, Aki and I would get invited to festivals in different parts of the world, and though that was always very exciting, in most cases we were really disappointed," Mika Kaurismäki explains. "They had very nice limousines, but they weren't Cadillacs. They put you in a nice room in a five-star hotel, but you had no contact with people. You'd know there were other filmmakers around but you'd never get to meet them. Once, in Toronto, security wouldn't even let me into my own party. I thought that would be the one place I wouldn't need an invitation."

Frustrated and thinking there must be a better way, the Kaurismäkis and fellow director Anssi Mänttäri came up with the idea to "do a festival in the middle of nowhere, where everyone would be in the same league and there wouldn't be any hierarchy." The brothers put in a quick call to some filmmaking friends ("We're doing this crazy festival, do you want to come?"), and the first year's guests were the impressive trio of Jonathan Demme, Bertrand Tavernier, and Sam Fuller, who grabbed Mika's arm so forcefully so many times that it was black-and-blue by the time the event ended.

Sitting in the bar attached to the Hotel Sodankyla, Mika Kourismäki, who met his wife, Finnish filmmaker Pia Tikka, in the Midnight Sun's "Grand Palais," knows some things have changed since 1986. "What's happening to me, I'm getting old," he mock grumbles. "Last night I went to sleep at 4 A.M., very early. During the first festival, I didn't sleep at all. For five days I only went to the movies."

Yet personal qualms notwithstanding, the director knows that the intensity of the Midnight Sun remains unchanged. "What makes this festival is our audience," he says. "They're very loyal and they make the atmosphere. They travel a day or whatever to get here, and they're coming to see movies. Thanks to the mosquitoes, everyone goes to the theaters. You can't escape the movies here." Attendees, Peter von Bagh adds, are "the best asset of the festival, a totally fascinated audience, not at all cynical."

Also unchanged is the rare chance festival-goers have to examine the careers of featured filmmakers in retrospective tributes. The Greek-born Costa-Gavras was here, as was the great Italian director Francesco Rosi. Seven of each man's films were shown (usually but not invariably with Finnish subtitles), including Rosi's exceptional 1963 *Hands over the City*, a corrosive study of urban political corruption that features a dubbed Rod Steiger nevertheless giving one of the best, most gripping performances of his career.

Just as gratifying was that both men, as well as German actress Angela Winkler (*The Lost Honor of Katharina Blum*, *The Tin Drum*), settled in for frank and leisurely two-hour extended public conversations with von Bagh in the high school gymnasium that started each festival day at 10 A.M. Costa-Gavras, maker of political melodramas like *Z* and *State of Siege*, was especially fascinating, revealing that the first film he saw as a boy was documentary footage of Mussolini and his mistress being killed, their bodies dragged down an Italian street. When, talking of his boyhood familiarity with American westerns, Costa-Gavras asked, "Do you know Randolph Scott?" Von Bagh promptly replied, "I knew him better than my own father."

In addition to everything else, at one time the Midnight Sun Festival eclectically focused on both 3-D and silent films, but the 3-D part of the event was temporarily dropped this year. "We've shown the available repertory," says von Bagh. "Now there is a break, I don't even know why."

In part to make up for that loss, there were two innovative silent programs in 1999, including Walter Ruttman's 1927 German classic *Berlin — Symphony of a Great City*, accompanied by Finnish percussionist Jouni Kesti. But the film everyone wanted to see, the most anticipated event of the entire festival in fact, was *Juha*, a brand-new silent film directed by, of all people, Aki Kaurismäki.

Though the Finnish Film Foundation newsletter headlined "Aki

Goes Silent" in big letters when this project was announced, the younger Kaurismäki brother, whose characters are usually dour and who's often said, von Bagh reported, "words are polluting our movies," did not make a completely unexpected move in deciding to do a modern silent film. His choice of subject was also intriguing: *Juha* is based on a novel by Juhani Aho, one of Finland's classic writers, a book that's already been filmed three times, starting with a 1920 version by Mauritz Stiller, the director best known as Greta Garbo's mentor.

Expecting a crush, especially because the nine-piece ensemble providing the music, the Ansii Tikanmaki Film Orchestra, were Midnight Sun favorites, the festival put *Juha* in its largest venue, the big Italian circus tent that holds roughly five hundred. Still, people lined up in the sunlight more than an hour before the 8:30 P.M. starting time and waited genially through another hour's technical delay, entertained by teenage circus-type performers, including a young woman on stilts, a two-person tiger, and a contortionist.

Once it unspooled, *Juha*'s story of a happily married Finnish farm wife who gets lured to the big city by an evil procurer turned out to be a match for the director's style. A touching homage to silent techniques that was both sincere and amusing, *Juha*, typically, demanded simultaneously to be taken seriously and not seriously at all.

Before *Juha* started, Aki Kaurismäki, who'd missed the festival's first few days, stood up at the front of the tent to introduce his film. With the completely expressionless attitude he favors, Aki used English to welcome everyone to "the screening of a lousy movie." Pointing to the screen and the orchestra, he added, "If you look up, there's a movie. If you look down, there's music. I prefer you look down." The applause was thunderous. It was a Midnight Sun moment, for sure.

PART THREE

Festivals with Aesthetic Agendas

Pordenone

Silent films have magic. They've outwitted history.

Once the most potent worldwide entertainment medium, silent films were subjected to a cultural firestorm of numbing proportions when sound came in. The prints themselves, according to Kevin Brownlow, the author of the landmark book *The Parade's Gone By* and a reigning authority on silent film, endured "a record of destruction worthy of Attila the Hun: they have burned them, dumped them in the sea, hacked the reels with axes, or let them rot in vaults."

Even the estimated 20 percent of films made between 1895 and the late 1920s that survived this physical purge were treated with disdain both calculated and accidental by those who screened them. James Card, another silent authority, said these films were often shown in "seventh generation, pallid dupes of 16 mm prints run at the wrong speed on a small screen and without music."

Or else the poor survivors were chopped up and played for cheap laughs, sliced and diced to feed the hungry maw of television. This happened to such an extent that, again according to Brownlow, "an entire generation of viewers has contempt for them, a prejudice so tremendous that even the creators themselves became terribly apologetic. At times I almost had to bully these people into watching their films with me."

Mocked, reviled, long considered dead and buried, silent film is going through a revival that is as remarkable as it is unexpected as a new generation of viewers comes to appreciate Brownlow's celebrated dictum that "it's hard to understand the last reel if you haven't seen the first." In one memorable week in Los Angeles, for instance, I had a choice of four separate silent programs, ranging from the familiar *Gold Rush* to the rarely seen Danish *Atlantis* to a disturbing Lon Chaney double bill and the western *The Covered Wagon*, all complete with live musical accompaniment.

And that music is quite unlike the indifferent piano tinkling of the TV years. Local symphonies have found accompanying silent film to be among their most popular activities: when Washington's National played for F.W. Murnau's *Nosferatu* at Wolf Trap, 5,649 tickets were sold, and for the Indianapolis Symphony with *The Phantom of the Opera*, 6,404 paid to get in.

In addition, new groups have been formed specifically to accompany silents. The inventive Cambridge-based Alloy Orchestra played their rich percussive score to the German *Sylvester* at the 1993 Telluride Film Festival, and their dynamism galvanized an overflow audience into cheering as if they'd witnessed a Beatles reunion. Five years later, in 1998, I was so excited by how beautifully matched their driving sound was to the factory setting of Sergei Eisenstein's classic *Strike* that I stood for most of the performance.

This silent revival is not a phenomenon limited to festivals or major cities. According to the *"Live" Cinema Calendar*, a thick monthly compilation of silents performed with music, showings take place in sites as nonmetropolitan as Coos Bay, Oregon, Saginaw, Michigan, and Bar Harbor, Maine. "The common reaction," says Tom Murray, the calendar's compiler, "is 'My god, I had no idea there was so much going on.'"

And for those living outside the wide range of live shows, there has been an eruption of silent film on video and cable, where the Turner Classic Movies channel has instituted a Silent Sunday Nights feature. The Library of Congress has combined with the Smithsonian Institution to produce a six-cassette series, "The Origins of American Film," showcasing rare early works, and companies like Kino on Video and Milestone Film & Video have dozens of silents available, everything from the familiar antics of Buster Keaton to the beautifully photographed action of the little-seen Maurice Tourner–Clarence Brown *Last of the Mohicans*. "There was zero market demand for these films thirty-five years ago," says Kino's Don Krim, while Milestone's Dennis Doros adds, "The interest in this area and the quality of the videos available have all gone way up in the past ten years."

While several factors have contributed to this revival, everyone involved agrees that one of the critical elements in the rebirth of silent films has been an annual event held not in New York, Los Angeles, London, or Paris but rather in a little-known Italian provincial capital of 50,000, a city with no previous connection to silent film located forty-five miles northeast of Venice at the foot of the Alps.

Every October since 1982, "Le Giornate del Cinema Muto," literally "The Days of Silent Film," has attracted visitors from places as distant as Japan, China, Israel, and India, as well as from all of Europe, to the prosperous, energetic but nontourist town of Pordenone—a combination of event and locale so unexpected that it's been characterized as "like having a festival on Amish quilting in Oklahoma."

So unlike other film gatherings it doesn't even want to be called a festival, Pordenone has become the nonpareil event of the silent film year, a place where a week of enthusiastic viewing starting at 9 A.M. daily and inevitably ending well after midnight leaves participants feeling, as Milestone's Doros put it, "like I'd spend seven days in heaven." With encomiums like this the rule not the exception, an Italian pilgrimage was unavoidable if I wanted to understand why vintage silent films were making a celebrated resurgence.

Part of an underappreciated region of Italy known as the Friuli and inhabited by, one guidebook realistically claims, "the warmest and most hospitable of the Italians," Pordenone has both elegant shops located on the cobblestoned Corso Vittorio Emanuele and the kind of cozy and welcoming restaurants you hate to leave. While the *New York Times* called the Friuli "home to one of the most refined food and wine cultures in the world," Pordenone, with but a handful of hotels within its limits, not only didn't rate any stars in the *Michelin Green Guide* to Italy, it was in fact dropped entirely from that magisterial volume in 1990.

Known a thousand years ago as Portus Naonis because of its function as a port on the River Noncello, Pordenone is now a manufacturing center, the home of Zanussi, Italy's biggest maker of appliances, considered to be the country's second largest industrial firm after Fiat.

Aside from the painting of sixteenth-century master and native son Giovanni Antonio de Sacchis, known to the world as "Il Pordenone," the closest the metropolis has gotten to any kind of fame is a backhanded mention in Ernest Hemingway's *A Farewell to Arms*. The great writer, who passed through the town as a World War I ambulance driver, was apparently not terribly impressed. He had a character dismiss it as "not much of a place" and in addition had his hero desert to Switzerland rather than retreat to its friendly confines. Not a ringing endorsement.

To its credit, however, Pordenone makes an excellent starting point for explorations of the rest of the Friuli, a region that has had three different capitals in its long history. Aquileia boasts a basilica with an enormous Roman mosaic floor, Udine a remarkable Venetian-style town square, and Cividale del Friuli the celebrated Tempietto Longobardo. This haunting, almost magical stucco relief of six maiden saints that sits on a high wall in a small temple by a rushing river has lost none of its mystery in the thousand years since the Lombards created it.

Back in Pordenone, with all screenings held at the creaky but endearing Teatro Verdi, a 1,200-seat opera theater dating from the early years of the century but given a 1950s remodeling replete with glass bricks and heavy curves, the Giornate traditionally elicits gasps of astonishment from the hundreds of visitors who gather for its pleasures.

The *Times* of London calls it "the annual miracle," and Edith Kramer, the current director of Berkeley's Pacific Film Archive, speaks for her fellow professionals, the people who already know the most about silent film, by saying, "This is where we go back to school, where we learn and are enriched in our own field. It's a privilege to attend, intense, intimate, a very special week."

As surprising as the festival's success is the unlikely reason for its existence, a massive 1976 earthquake that devastated the entire Friuli region and practically leveled Gemona, hometown of a pair of married film buffs named Livio Jacob (now Pordenone's chairman) and Piera Patat.

Both students in Trieste, the couple had their interest in movies intensified by membership in a film society run by journalist Lorenzo Codelli. Through Codelli, they met the late Angelo R. Humouda, a legendary politically committed film archivist who until his death traveled throughout Italy in a green Volkswagen van jammed with silent films, early cartoons, and a projector, exhibiting his treasures to audiences that wouldn't ordinarily be exposed to them.

Strong regional partisans (Patat likes to wear a "Friulani Are Fabulous" button), the couple wanted to do something for their area, perhaps raise money to rebuild Gemona's destroyed movie theaters. They consulted with Humouda, who instead volunteered to bring his traveling silents to Gemona, which he did in 1977. And he offered some astute advice.

"He told us, 'with the little money you can raise, you won't ever be able to build a theater, but you can buy films,'" Patat remembers. "He introduced us to a world completely new to us, the world of American 16 mm distributors."

The couple began buying films, eventually founding an archive in Gemona called La Cineteca del Friuli. They became friendly with Paolo Cherci Usai, a colleague of Humouda's, and Piero Colussi and Andrea Crozzoli of Cinemazero, a film society with a theater in nearby Pordenone. In 1982, the group decided to put on a retrospective of the French silent comic Max Linder in Pordenone. Though the gathering didn't even have a name, and any thoughts of making it an annual event would have seemed preposterous, this was the first Pordenone Festival. There were only eight guests.

While the Pordenone committee (later joined by historian Davide Turconi and technical expert Carlo Montanaro and still later by critic David Robinson) was feeling its way, great changes were taking place in the silent film world. The most important was the international acclaim that greeted the 1980 screening of Kevin Brownlow's twenty-years-in-the-making reconstruction of Abel Gance's monumental *Napoleon*, accompanied by a specially written Carmine Coppola score.

"It filled Radio City Music Hall in New York for ten days," remembers Kino's Don Krim, still amazed. "It showed the possibility of what silent films could be to every theater owner, distributor, critic, and moviegoer." Anyone who experienced riding the huge wave of audience emotion when the multi-hour film reached its climax as the screen opened to three times its normal size and Bonaparte's revolutionary army marched into Italy counts it as one of their most intense moviegoing memories.

One of the things that *Napoleon*'s success demonstrated was the importance of being fanatical about showing silents in as authentic conditions as possible. In addition to procuring the best possible prints (especially important because the photographic quality of the originals couldn't be more different from the grainy, pathetic copies often seen today), this meant paying close attention to a pair of factors — projection speed and musical accompaniment — whose neglect had led directly to the way silents had dwindled in popularity.

For though there is a uniform sound projection speed of 24 frames per second, nothing of the kind exists for silent films, largely because they were shot by cinematographers who hand-cranked their cameras. They speeded up or slowed down the movement from film to film and even within films from 16 frames per second to 20-something per second as the action dictated.

Making things even more complicated is that footage was often supposed to be projected faster than it was shot, ensuring that stunts looked crisper and slapstick funnier. Speeds also varied with decades, and projecting D. W. Griffith's ambitious 1916 epic *Intolerance* at the late silent speed of 24 frames per second instead of the intended 16 to 18 makes it play like comedy, while showing 1927's gently romantic *Sunrise* at 16 frames per second instead of the intended 24 has the unfortunate tendency, says Kevin Brownlow, "to put audiences to sleep."

Though modern silent projectionists don't generally change the tempo within films, they must have a knowledge of what the standard frames-per-second count was in each of the films they show plus the ability to work with today's breed of variable speed projectors. The aim remains what it was in 1911, when a practitioner wrote that the ideal projectionist is someone who "'renders' a film, if he is a real operator, exactly as does the musician render a piece of music, in that, within limits, the action of a scene being portrayed depends entirely on his judgment."

Music overall was a much more central element of presentation than modern audiences realize, accounting for what is generally conceded to be 50 percent of a given film's impact. The most prestigious films had specially composed music (Saint-Saëns wrote an early score) played by musicians with impressive credentials: according to one count, there were as many as five hundred orchestras working the biggest theaters, ranging in size from twenty-six to ninety players and coping with music of such complexity that the original score for D. W. Griffith's *Way Down East* contained 242 tempo changes. But no theater, no matter how humble, ever considered showing films without at least a piano player or organist, who, if he or she didn't have a full score or at least musical guidelines to work with, would be called upon to improvise on what was seen on screen.

"Most silent films were 80 percent emotional and 20 percent intellectual. That's not meant as a slap; it's the way they were constructed," said William Everson, one of the deans of silent film history. "The score minimized flaws, added punctuation and feeling, stretched the emotionalism and guided the audience into the right frame of mind. It's a major crime, absolutely deadly, to show these films without the proper accompaniment."

And, as Kevin Brownlow wrote, because "they were the movies until sound came in, calling them silent suggests they were lacking something"—many partisans wince whenever that term is used. James Card, in his appreciative memoir *Seductive Cinema*, goes so far as to refer to "speechless cinema" and "predialogue, so-called silent film," so deep is his passion for the art that is no more.

The rediscovery and reconstruction of *Napoleon* not only showed the commercial potential of correctly presented silent movies, it also symbolized the most surprising aspect of the art's revival. Pictures long thought to be lost forever, key works unseen for decades and written off as victims of nitrate film stock's inevitable physical disintegration, were turning up on a regular basis, uncovered in places ranging from an abandoned swimming pool in the Yukon to the basement of a Danish tavern where Peter the Great once spent the night.

One of the great Japanese silents, Teinosuke Kinugasa's 1926 *A Page of Madness*, the hallucinatory tale of an old man who works at the asylum where his wife is confined with the hope of freeing her, was found in a rice barrel in the garden of the director's country house. *The Last of the Duanes*, a celebrated Tom Mix western, was discovered under layers of bird excrement on the floor of a chicken farm building in a remote Czech village. And the actor James Mason came across many of Buster Keaton's personal 35 mm prints lying neglected in the garage of the comedian's former home.

Private collectors, a group so large that Pordenone's Paolo Cherci Usai calls them "a galaxy beyond our imagination," tend to be similarly reticent about their film holdings because possession of copyrighted films from an illegitimate source is illegal. And, as James Card notes dryly, "The FBI has not been shy about swooping down on private film collections and carrying them off." But other discoveries, paradoxically enough, began to come out of places that had legal rights to their films but didn't know exactly what they had.

Those would be state-run archives in far corners of the world, places like Australia and the former Czechoslovakia that had been terminal points in studio distribution systems that were so lackadaisical about what they were shipping out they didn't think it was worth the return postage to have anything sent back.

But though these archives have prints in huge numbers (the National Film and Sound Archive of Australia recently returned more than 1,600 American films to this country), literally decades can go by before they get the money and the manpower to actually examine their holdings. "It's mind-boggling what it takes in terms of labor to look at entire films," says the PFA's Edith Kramer, and Kevin Brownlow adds, "Archives are ludicrously underfunded. If they'd take the budgets on about twelve of these TV movies they could save an entire era."

With all the ingredients for a silent film revival in place, from this continual rediscovery of important films to an understanding of how to present them, what was most needed was a spot to bring it all together — which is where Pordenone fortuitously entered the picture.

"I swear we had no idea it would ever be like this," says a harried Paolo Cherci Ursai, who is now curator of the prestigious George Eastman film archive in Rochester, New York, as well as a member of the Pordenone committee. "The first festival was a group of friends, not even a convention in the American sense. But as soon as we put this together, the speed with which people came was amazing, as if they were waiting for this to happen. It was the right thing at the right time — and in the right place. This wouldn't have become what it has in a big city like Paris; it would have been absorbed and disappeared in a hundred other things."

What Pordenone did from the start was display the field's best work to those who could best appreciate it, an essential task because, preservationists being human, there is not much impetus to do a great job of restoration if there is nowhere to take a bow. And since, explains Paolo Cherci Usai, "we put the spotlight on, if it makes a splash in Pordenone, it will make a splash everywhere." Both collectors and archives worldwide find themselves thinking, in Kevin Brownlow's words, "What can we dig up, what can we do for Pordenone this year?"

As a result, there is rarely an archive or private collector that can't be prevailed upon to contribute prints; more than forty different sources were credited in 1994's program. This leads to both an unmatched completeness in the festival's retrospectives and the periodic appearance of one-of-a-kind rarities. Brownlow, for instance, is still talking about the 16 mm home movie footage an Italian tourist shot of Buster Keaton filming *The Cameraman* on the streets of New York that a collector brought to the Verdi screen one year.

Furthermore, says Paolo Cherci Usai, since Pordenone "refuses to obey the logic of the masterpiece," the festival also delights in showing "bad films that have slept on the shelves for eighty years, that no one dared to touch." Pordenone even has a section where unknown films are screened for audience identification: one year, remembers Lorenzo Codelli, the great Italian director Sergio Leone literally leapt out of his seat at the shock of recognizing an early film starring his own father, actor/director Vincenzo Leone.

Essential to Pordenone's success is the festival's most intangible quality: an unpretentious warmth that I felt from the moment I arrived. While most festivals pride themselves on scheduling more films than anyone could possibly see, making sleep difficult and meals impossible, Pordenone is a human-scale event, gracefully combining comprehensiveness with the conviviality of an intimate family.

Yes, this is a serious international gathering, but it retains a charming Mickey-and-Judy-putting-on-a-show energy, and it has enough respect for life's noncinematic pleasures to build in the kind of two-and-a-half-hour breaks for lunch and dinner that visitors to Italy will appreciate. And Pordenone itself turned out to be enough of a small town to encourage art students to compete in decorating local shop windows with displays incorporating the festival's Buster Keaton–inspired logo.

Holding the festival almost exclusively in one theater may seem like a small thing, but anyone who has spent frantic hours at other festivals first trying to figure out which of several conflicting films to see and then rushing around trying to get from one venue to another knows what bliss a single setting is. And because the Pordenone area's finite hotel space limits the number of out-of-towners who can attend, lining up ahead of time to assure a decent seat, the bane of most festivals, is unheard of.

Run by the still-youthful zealots who were present at the creation and with its eager participants exuding an atmosphere of backpack academia ("a sort of Woodstock of silent cinema," said one bearded regular), Pordenone is completely in love with the purity of what is on the screen. There is no A list, no glitz, no glamour; "all the stars belonging to this world," someone said to me, "are dead." I did have a scare one morning, when I spotted a flock of limousines and video cameras at the Verdi, but they turned out to be drawn by a wedding in the hotel across the street, not a celebrity encounter.

"We're the same group of people. We've never forgotten the way the whole thing started, and we don't want to change," emphasizes Paolo Cherci Usai. "And though we're so different culturally and personally that our meetings can be like volcanoes exploding, no one wants to break the magic by leaving."

The collegial atmosphere at Pordenone is more than just pleasant, it makes what the festival does possible. For one of the characteristics that participants agree marks this gathering as unique is that it's the only place where all branches of the often-fractious silent film community declare a truce and fraternize with the enemy.

Arcane as it is, the silent film world is as rife with turf wars as any inner city neighborhood. Collectors scorn archivists as unduly cautious and conservative, while archivists return the favor by looking down on private enthusiasts as little more than freebooters who don't take proper care of their holdings. Even academics and archivists have their differences, the former angry at not being able to get the access they want and the latter upset because use inevitably damages their prints.

Pordenone, says Paolo Cherci Usai, is "the only place where you can meet everybody. Archivists, semiologists, the guy crazy for Louise Fazenda, they all want to come here, they're all equal here, with no sense of authority." And they are so determined to see every available frame that not even Pordenone's biggest public demonstration in more than twenty years, part of a one-day nationwide general strike in 1994, could lure anyone out of the Verdi except me.

Because what archives and collectors bring to Pordenone is the newly found and the unexpected (often adding previously unknown or under-appreciated films like Frank Borzage's 1929 *Lucky Star*, the surprise hit of the 1990 event, to the list of accepted masterpieces), the festival has developed a reputation for what is called canon-busting, for shaking up everyone's ideas of what is significant and why. Pordenone, says historian David Shepard with appropriate drama (this is the movies, after all), "takes the chains off film bibles throughout the world. There are all kinds of films I had no idea were important until I saw them here."

The example at the top of everyone's list is Pordenone's 1989 explo-ration of prerevolutionary Russian cinema, specifically the films of direc-tor Evgenii Bauer. Unexpectedly sophisticated works that had not been seen outside their country of origin since 1917 and were thought destroyed, Bauer's productions were characterized by technical innova-tions, a subtle, Chekovian sense of character, and the dramatic use of light and shadow. "There was the exhilaration of discovery," wrote David Robinson in *Sight & Sound*, "a vision of marvellous vistas — but also an awesome sense of the vast interior that remains to be explored."

The uproar in 1994 was not quite so intense, but as always the festi-val was bookended by a pair of special screenings with full musical scores that were specially commissioned for the occasion. Opening night was *Lonesome*, a naturalistic late silent from 1928 directed by Paul Fejos and accompanied by a captivating score by the Alloy Orchestra, the crowd-pleasers from Telluride. A simple but enchanting Manhattan love story about a man and a woman (Glenn Tryon and Barbara Kent) who find each other during a raucous day at Coney Island only to nearly lose everything, it elicited sighs of satisfaction as it went up and down real roller-coasters as well as the emotional kind.

Closing night struck quite a different note. *The Unknown*, directed by the brooding Tod Browning in 1927, starred Lon Chaney as a circus performer who pretends to be armless and Joan Crawford as the ingenue who likes him that way. It was so unnerving that even John Cale, who wrote and performed the ultramodern electronic score, was moved to call it "a fairly sick film, for want of a better word."

The biggest aural surprise was the intoxicating Indian music, a combination of vocals, percussion, and harmonium improvised on the spot by a pickup group of European-based Indian musicians for a selection of silents that had never left the subcontinent before. I found myself going to more Indian films than I'd planned on, just to hear the hypnotic instrumental interplay. The best of the lot was a stunning print of the 1928 *Shiraz*, an assured Oriental fantasy about the building of the Taj Mahal that featured everything from toothless soothsayers to execution by elephant's foot.

The festival's other main series featured Hollywood work that had never before been gathered together with such painstaking thoroughness, like the silent westerns of William Wyler, collected from eight sources scattered around the world and accompanied by rugged, indefatigable piano players who relieved each other at two-hour intervals. In a classic Pordenone touch, at the conclusion of the last Wyler shown, the spirited, sweeping *Hell's Heroes*, which has protagonist Charles Bickford crawling into a church as the congregation sings "Silent Night," a local Pordenone choir sneaked into the Verdi and sang several choruses of that hymn to great effect.

The films I looked forward to most were the elegant and sophisticated features from little-known, unaccountably forgotten director Monta Bell, who combined a sardonic sense of humor with surprising emotional subtlety and poignance. A typical moment, from *Lady of the Night*, had a hard-boiled Norma Shearer getting out of prison and casually checking her makeup in the shiny body of a passing hearse. It was hard not to be won over by the cool audacity of it all.

At the other end of the spectrum was the slapstick gang, well over a hundred comic shorts from obscure performers drawn together under the rubric "Forgotten Laughter: Unknown American Comedians." Most popular of these was the eccentric Jewish comic Max Davidson, whose elaborate shrugs of resignation at increasingly ridiculous situations had audiences saluting him as Woody Allen's cinematic grandfather. His *Pass the Gravy* was voted Le Giornate's most popular comedy short, and had everyone in the Verdi truly convulsed.

Experiencing the total immersion of Pordenone, seeing these films as originally intended, makes inescapable the truth of what fans have continually maintained: silent film is a vivid world all its own. As historian William Everson insists, "This was not a shoddy little flickering art medium, not the primitive forerunner of anything. This deserves to be seen as a completely separate art, something unique and full blown."

Key to this view is to realize and accept that the absence of spoken dialogue is not a handicap to endure but a virtue to enjoy. For the hidden, unexpected pleasure of silent films is the way they seduce audiences into becoming, in the most modern way, full interactive participants in the movie experience. "You're not told what to think or feel," explains Michael Friend of the Academy of Motion Picture Arts and Sciences. "A kind of emotional space is produced which is open for you to enter, a space for reflection between the film and the music."

To understand what that means, it helps to recall one of the most famous scenes in silent film history, the moment in 1925's *The Phantom of the Opera* when Mary Philbin's mischievous Christine reaches around and removes the mask covering Lon Chaney's face. By virtue of a clever camera angle we see the Phantom's horrific visage before Christine does, in dreamy repose for an instant and then, unforgettably, in agony as the creature realizes that his dreams of acceptance and love are over. It is a moment of supreme emotion, one of the greatest the silent world has to offer, and because no speech is heard, nothing distracts or distances us from directly experiencing its shock. Because we are on our own, without words to guide or straitjacket us, we are in effect meeting the scene halfway, unavoidably filling it up with our own strong feelings.

Paradoxically underlining the difference between sound and silence was the 1994 festival's opening night screening of *Lonesome*, shown in a version to which some brief spoken inserts had been added once sound became all the rage. The sophisticated emotions the dialogueless sequences evoked were shattered when the actors could actually be heard. For while sound particularizes, silence turns out to universalize, allowing the audience to share completely in the on-screen dream. No one spending time at Pordenone could fail to agree with Mary Pickford's famous statement: "It would have been more logical if silent pictures had grown out of the talking instead of the other way around."

If there is a downside to the story of Le Giornate de Cinema Muto it is that, like Italy itself, the festival always seems to be on the brink of falling victim to economic and logistical pressures. Though its roughly $400,000 annual cost is tiny (about as much, it has been said, as a single morning at the flashier Venice Film Festival), Pordenone has been more appreciated internationally than at home and never quite knows how or if it is going to cover its expenses. Its proximity to the nearby NATO base at Aviano has made hotel rooms perennially difficult to reserve. And the quasi-crumbling Teatro Verdi is always in danger of being closed for the kind of renovations that could take years to finish and possibly take the heart out of the proceedings.

(In 1999, when uncertainty about whether the Verdi would be restored or demolished and replaced by a new theater reached new heights, the Giornate moved less than ten miles down the road to the town of Sacile, "the Garden of Venice," located on a natural island formed by the river Livenza. Screenings were held in the 1911 Teatro Zancanaro, which fortuitously reopened in 1997 after renovations lasting nearly a decade.)

Pordenone, obviously, is not about to give up. For one thing, it means too much to its participants. One film historian told of a colleague who insisted on coming though he was close to death: "It was extraordinary, that visit, as if he just wanted to see Mecca before he died." It is no wonder then that Paolo Cherci Usai, speaking passionately for the entire committee, says, "It's a moral commitment, not a job. They will really have to kill us to kill the festival. They will have to walk on our corpses to cause us to disappear."

Lone Pine

Ask not what the world can do for you, says the self-sufficient Lone Pine Film Festival, show everyone what you've done for the world.

While the standard festival looks outward, offering itself as a place where movies from everywhere can find a home, the folks here turn that formula on its head, inviting visitors to celebrate what this tiny Eastern Sierra town three hours from Los Angeles has contributed to the universe of film.

In what has been called the most focused movie event in the world, the Lone Pine Film Festival, which began in 1990, concentrates exclusively on motion pictures shot in the harsh and craggy landscape of the unique Alabama Hills just outside of town. Even pretenders that were lensed only sixty miles away in Bishop are righteously excluded.

Named after a notable tree that was uprooted in a storm more than a hundred years ago, Lone Pine is known today as the gateway to Mount Whitney, the highest peak in the contiguous forty-eight states. That makes it attractive to so many European tourists that Jake's Saloon on Main Street has to have signs in three languages informing visitors of the state's liquor laws.

Isolated though it is (nearby Kirkwood advertises itself as the place where visitors "Rub Shoulders with No One"), Lone Pine is connected to several strands of California history. Located in the heart of the Owens Valley, it had its water supply seized decades ago by impudent Los Angeles in an action (dramatized in Robert Towne's script for Roman Polanski's *Chinatown*) that still rankles locally. Also, the Manzanar War Relocation Center, where Japanese Americans were forcibly interned during World War II, is just up the road.

But as far as festival-goers are concerned, Lone Pine is celebrated for at least three hundred motion pictures that were shot here over a seventy-five-year period. These range from not-surprising efforts like *Bad Day at Black Rock* and *High Sierra* (which featured Humphrey Bogart careening down Whitney Portal Road just outside of town) to more unexpected titles.

Because of their singular topography and proximity to Hollywood, the Alabama Hills have stood in for everything from the Andes in the John Wayne–starring *Tycoon* to the wilds of Tibet in *The Shadow* and even another universe in *Star Trek V*. Most memorably, director George Stevens and company spent three months here shooting the classic *Gunga Din* in areas that look so much like the hill country of India's Northwest Frontier that Indian friends of star Douglas Fairbanks Jr. insisted they knew exactly where on the subcontinent it had been filmed.

More recently, commercials and videos have monopolized the landscape, with companies coming from as far away as Germany, Finland, and Japan and celebrities like Michael Jordan (for Gatorade) and Willie Nelson and Waylon Jennings (for Pizza Hut) getting comfortable in the scenery.

Mostly, however, they shot westerns in Lone Pine, westerns, westerns, and more westerns. And though some prestige items such as *How the West Was Won* and parts of the Mel Gibson–starring *Maverick* were lensed here, more often it was the sturdy and unpretentious B westerns that used the site, with cowboys such as Tom Mix, Hoot Gibson, Ken Maynard, and Tim Holt being invited to saddle up.

Both Robert Mitchum and Roy Rogers had their first starring roles in

Lone Pine, Gene Autry filmed sixteen pictures here, and William Boyd made thirty-two Hopalong Cassidy epics. Director Budd Boetticher shot several of his elegiac 1960s westerns starring Randolph Scott such as *The Tall T* and *Ride Lonesome* in the area, and it was the site of John Wayne's last filmed appearance, a 1978 commercial for California-based Great Western Savings & Loan.

Given all of this, no one should be surprised that Lone Pine has a distinctly western flavor to it. When I visited in 1995, the festival saluted Gene Autry, "America's Favorite Cowboy," but since Autry was too infirm to attend, the title of grand marshal of the Sunday afternoon parade went to a more unconventional choice. That was eighty-eight-year-old Pierce Lyden, a quintessential bad guy in black hat and pencil mustache who appeared in literally hundreds of B westerns and first worked in Lone Pine back in 1937.

More than knowing their B westerns backward and forward, festivalgoers also know how to dress the part. When I walked onto the town's Main Street for the opening night party, I felt the eerie, anachronistic sensation that goes with hearing the surprisingly delicate but unmistakable jingle of spurs as dozens of revelers in full western gear wandered by, drinks in hand.

For one of Lone Pine's functions is to provide people who are not shy about confessing how major an impact western films have had on their lives the opportunity to do some serious dressing up. Joe "Hoppy" Sullivan, a district sales manager from Cicero, Indiana, spent years studying still photographs of Hopalong Cassidy with a magnifying glass and wears a beautiful costume that reflects that concern. And Ermal Williamson of Van Nuys, California, has an unexpected job description: he's a professional John Wayne impersonator who has even performed weddings as the Duke.

Visitors like these come to Lone Pine in such numbers they just about double the town's usual population of 2,000 and so strain the hotel room situation for miles around that Dave Holland, the festival's affable director says, "Where I'm at now is I need a bigger town."

Simultaneously bemused and proud of being the focus of this kind of worshipful attention, the residents of Lone Pine work to make the festival a city-wide event. Local businesses allow their windows to be painted with portraits of cowboy heroes and make room for photographs of Saturday matinee stars next to signs that read "Yes We Have Steer Manure." Both the VFW and the American Legion throw pancake breakfasts, the Lions Club provides a "Western Deep-Pit BBQ," and everyone lines Main Street for Sunday's hometown parade, complete with fire engines, dogs with bandanas, and the Inyo County Board of Supervisors.

Though the twenty-plus Lone Pine movies shown in 16 mm in the local high school auditorium are always a draw, the festival has other, equally down-home attractions. Veteran stunt man Loren James, who doubled for Steve McQueen for twenty-two years, shows his action reel, a panel discussion allows visitors to question visiting stars such as Peggy Stewart, "Queen of the Republic Westerns," and a dealers' area encourages purchase of hundreds of western videos and such oddities as an edible reproduction of Hopalong Cassidy's belt buckle — in either milk or dark chocolate.

Inevitably — and this is something that gives the Lone Pine event a haunting, indelible quality — what draws most festival-goers is exactly the same thing that brought all those movie companies to the area in the first place: the chance to wander around one of California's least-known and most extraordinary natural phenomena, the Alabama Hills.

Even though I'd seen them repeatedly on film, the actual sight of these enormous, grandiose boulders, stretched out in bewildering groupings like giant gumdrops randomly sprinkled over the landscape by a playful higher power, was genuinely breathtaking. These weathered granite rocks, once erroneously thought to be "the oldest hills in the world" and named by southern Civil War sympathizers after a Confederate battleship, give off an otherworldly aura, so much so that I felt almost frightened to be in their midst. My mind spun fantasy after fantasy, until it seemed plausible to view the outcroppings as somehow huddled together for companionship, warmth, and understanding, like the outcast "Freaks" of Todd Browning's movie. If someone had told me these stones were once alive on another planet, or at the very least housed an H. P. Lovecraft–type alien, unknowable civilization, I wouldn't have doubted it.

The first Hollywood production to find its way to Lone Pine was a 1920 Fatty Arbuckle film called *The Roundup*. Film companies got to like it here partially because the local citizenry treated everyone like family, even building a hotel called the Dow (I stayed in the more modern annex) for their comfort. But mostly filmmakers returned again and again because of the wide variety of looks the Alabama Hills provided. Director Boetticher, a visitor so often "I should have been elected mayor long ago," spoke for his colleagues when he told a BBC interviewer, "The great thing about Lone Pine is that you don't need to go anywhere else. It looks like they built these mountains for the movies."

Equally enthusiastic about the locale are fans like the gentleman who flew in from Brazil one year and took a soon-to-be-legendary $300 cab ride directly from Los Angeles International Airport to the festival. Or people like Ian Whitcomb, author and entertainer and host of his own Los Angeles–area radio show, who'd watched Lone Pine movies as a boy in Britain and thought "maybe all of America looks like this."

Unable to track down the location once he came to the United States, Whitcomb stumbled on the hills, as many people do, on a drive back from the ski areas of Mammoth. "I suddenly realized I was in my dream," Whitcomb told me, wonder still in his voice. "I was in the America I'd always wanted to be in but never found. In fact, the whole of the dream the rest of the world got of America was contained in the Alabama Hills."

Since the hills are owned by the federal government and administered by the Department of Interior's Bureau of Land Management, they have the advantage of looking just as they did when all that filming took place. "Everything else has been mutilated," says Mike Johnson, a B western fan who works for Lloyds of London in Toronto, shaking his head at the waste. "Only this location remains exactly as it was sixty years ago." Or, as festival director Dave Holland frequently explains, the hills are "a living museum."

Holland, a gregarious, still boyish man of middle years, is a former publicist and journalist who enjoys saying things like "I'll try not to blow smoke in your ear" and "There's no law against being friendly." He took over the festival, which was founded by Lone Pine resident Kerry Powell, in its second year. And because he is a self-described "location freak" who has been exploring the Alabama Hills for thirty years, he was instrumental in giving the event its unique character.

Location freaks, explains Holland, are people who "want to stand where their heroes stood, who think it's exciting to take a photo from a film and say, 'By god, that's the same rock, do you realize what happened here?' It sounds naive to want to relive a myth, but that's what it is."

For Holland, what that means first of all is keeping his eye on the scenery, not the plot, when he watches a vintage movie. Then, accompanied by batches of stills, he's tirelessly walked around the Alabamas, off and on for years with particular photos, examining the lines and contours of the rocks and hoping to match the picture to the location.

Having documented his findings in a book and video called, not surprisingly, *On Location in Lone Pine*, Holland was the driving force in setting up a range of tours of the Alabamas (there now are six different ones to choose from) that are the festival's most popular aspect. And at each stop on every tour, visitors get to see stills from the relevant movies attached to pedestals planted exactly where the original movie cameras stood. It gives you chills, it really does.

Going on tour with the contagiously enthusiastic Holland is invariably an energizing experience. He charges through the sagebrush, exclaiming, "Look at that!" while he points out, not for the first time, the small piles of rocks that anchored the famous *Gunga Din* suspension bridge. And when Holland introduces locales like the cucumber-shaped Gene Autry rock, used in everything from Autry's *Boots and Saddle* to

Lives of a Bengal Lancer, it is easy to feel with him when he says happily, "This is hallowed ground."

All this points to Lone Pine's unusual place in the film festival cosmos. Turning its back on today, it devotes itself to as mythic a genre as cinema history has. And unlike, say, the world of silents, westerns and adventure epics are films that festival-goers experienced firsthand while they were thriving, and most likely in the impressionable years of childhood. Being brought back to that world, being able to actually walk around in unforgettable scenery that seemed the very stuff of fantasy when first we saw it, is a heady experience indeed.

If there is anybody besides Holland who represents the spirit of Lone Pine it is parade grand marshal Pierce Lyden. Clear-eyed and goodhumored at eighty-eight, he casually leaned against a hotel fence post while talking to me, speaking with easy grace and bemusement about a life both in and out of pictures that sounded as authentic and distant as if Buffalo Bill himself were standing next to me.

"I was born and raised in a sod house on a ranch in western Nebraska with no fences, no telephone, no electricity," Lyden remembers. "My dad bought horses for the cavalry, and I was handling cattle and breaking horses by the time I was eleven or twelve."

Determined to act, Lyden began on the stage but left it for Hollywood once the talkies came in. "Since I could do my own riding and stunt work, they didn't have to double me," he says. "The people who made the B westerns, we did a job, we went home, and we thought that was the end. We never thought they'd be remembered like they are today."

Going almost directly from Lone Pine to a western film festival in London, Pierce Lyden, who never got to wear a white hat, still can't quite believe all the attention that is being paid to his career. "The old bad man is the grand marshal," he says, shaking his head and smiling to himself. "They must be getting to the bottom of the barrel."

Telluride

More than twenty-two years ago, powered by the energy of youth, an innocent critic ventured out from the East Coast to a small festival in Colorado, then in just its third year. This is what he wrote:

"Telluride is the name whispered to you as you sit shivering from celluloid overdose in a café in Cannes. Go to Telluride, the voices say, only a few years old and already the most respected small film festival in the world. Telluride is different, the voices say, and for once the voices are right."

The words are mine, and when a considerably larger and more established Telluride recently celebrated its twenty-fifth anniversary with a gala five-day event (up from the usual four), the temptation to reexamine what London's *Sunday Times* has called "one of the US's most exclusive arts events" was hard to avoid.

Today's Telluride combines worthy new films, in-person tributes to cinema grandees, and exclusive showings of venerable rarities. Most people who make the trek to this remote western town seven hours from Denver experience varying degrees of ecstasy, praising the festival as artistically adventurous and iconoclastic. Even unlikely visitors like action director Renny Harlin told an audience he'd turned to producing (he came with his debut, *Ramblin Rose*) because "I knew that as a director I'd never get invited to Telluride."

But Telluride was not always the way it appears now, and it doesn't necessarily call forth the same responses from all its visitors. Over its quarter-of-a-century lifespan the festival has made an almost personal journey from lionized darling to the focus of questions and doubts to its current position as a battle-scarred but still idealistic survivor in an increasingly commercialized world. "We live on such a tenuous edge between survival and extinction," says festival general manager Stella Pence, "that tiny factors become tidal waves." The ways Telluride has chosen to ride out those waves find echoes in my own varying levels of enthusiasm toward festivals in general and this singular one in particular.

The most obvious differences between Telluride then and Telluride now are, predictably, the surface ones, the inevitable results of celebrity, prosperity, and the passage of time. In 1976, you could buy a general festival ticket for $65 and an economy one for $35; today, a regular Telluride pass is $500, and the fast-selling patron passes run $2,500. The festival's first outlay was an almost invisible $8,300; today, it's $1.8 million, the size of the total annual budget for the local school system.

Instead of the one theater it began with, the restored 1914 Sheridan Opera House, the festival now has seven, five of which have to be built anew every year inside existing structures and then taken down. The theatrical building blocks, from seats to speakers, spend the off-season in rural Colorado inside large trailers with the festival's slogan "Show" painted on the sides.

Where food was once a catch-as-catch-can activity, Telluride, now with as many volunteers (close to five hundred) as it once had visitors, has to help out oversubscribed local restaurants by making extensive plans to supply its own people with an estimated 20,000 meals.

"The executive chef from the Putney Inn in Vermont brings in her staff and sets up an entire feeding operation," says Stella Pence. "She comes to town in early June, visits the local farmers to tell them what we need, they plant and harvest it, and we give them the leftovers back as mulch. It's its own weird little cottage industry."

"Wouldn't it be nice to build a festival where the theaters were already there, a place where there would be restaurants?" Stella's husband, Bill Pence, one of the festival's permanent codirectors, wistfully adds. "This is not like the festivals at Sundance or Toronto, which get all kinds of resources from the town. We pay as we go, like a taxi."

As for the town itself, anyone who's slept through the past quarter century would hardly recognize anything about it except its celebrated location 8,750 feet high in the San Juan Mountains of southwestern Colorado, where the oxygen pressure is 40 percent lower than at sea level, smack at the end of a dead-end road leading into a spectacular box canyon.

Just about a ghost town when the festival started, with a population of only a few hundred, Telluride, especially after a nerve-racking small airport (the world's second-highest commercial facility) opened just outside town in 1985, has boomed into an example of what's alternately called the Aspenification or the Californication of the state. As one reporter tartly put it a few years ago, "A sleepy haven for aging hippies is now a boom town of condos, million-dollar houses and billion dollar ski resorts."

In 1976, the Telluride I wrote about was "a pleasant, if slightly unreal fantasy town, where 70 percent of the population is thirty-five or under, a live-in Disneyland for people who never want to go home anymore." A place where drug dealing was legendary and local phones had only four digits as late as 1989, Telluride now is overshadowed by Mountain Village, a big deal collection of costly trophy homes and ski resorts, located up the mountain a gondola ride away from downtown.

Where dirt and gravel roads were once the norm and entire city blocks could probably have been bought for $10,000, even Telluride's back streets have just been blacktopped because, says one bemused resident, "if you've got million dollar shacks, you've got to pave the alleys." In fact, snow-loving celebrities like Tom Cruise, Keith Carradine,

Sylvester Stallone, and Oprah Winfrey have places here, and Oliver Stone just sold his for an impressive $8 million.

Paralleling these changes and in some way reflecting them are the more important differences in how the festival has been perceived over time by the international film world. To understand those, it's helpful to start from the premise that the hothouse filmcentric universe Telluride creates over a Labor Day weekend has always been more a religion than anything as ordinary as a festival, complete with messianic believers and agnostic scoffers.

When Telluride began in 1973, Sundance did not exist, and neither did Toronto, currently the Bigfoot of North America's fall film events. Where well under a hundred festivals were then in business worldwide, now there are several times as many, including a number in Colorado. "The difference is huge," says codirector Bill Pence. "The whole thing's become an industry."

None of this was so much as a dream in the early 1970s, when the Pences ran the classics-oriented distributor Janus Films and, living in Ridgeway, Colorado, programmed two local opera houses, the Sheridan in nearby Telluride and the Wheeler in Aspen.

In 1972, the Pences and James Card, then curator of films at Eastman House in Rochester, New York, brought a pair of silent pictures to the Sheridan. "The town was filled with refugees from the '60s," remembers Stella Pence. "They gave us a wonderful reception. We were all so excited, we decided to do a festival there the next year, a one-time deal. We didn't start with any ideal. It was just, 'Let's have a party.'"

With a tribute to controversial German director Leni Riefenstahl attracting media attention, Telluride, with Card and Tom Luddy (then director of Berkeley's Pacific Film Archive) serving as codirectors with Bill Pence, was immediately successful. Luddy (now a producer whose credits include *Mishima*, *The Secret Garden*, and *My Family*), remains as a permanent codirector with Pence, but after Card and his successor and fellow silent film expert William Everson left, a system of using serious film buffs and scholars as one-year guest directors was instituted.

Judged by its often lurid past, Telluride was not a likely place for something as peaceful as a festival to flourish. Likely named after tellurium, a nonmetallic element often found combined with more prestigious ores, Telluride began as a mining town in the 1870s, and its mountains, which once yielded millions in gold, silver, copper, lead, and zinc, are still laced with enough miles of tunnels to extend from Los Angeles to San Francisco.

With a population reaching 5,000 and calling itself "The Town without a Belly Ache" because it was too prosperous to complain, Telluride, often a violent place, was the site of an 1889 escapade (the looting of the San Miguel National Bank of $24,580) by the man who went on to call himself Butch Cassidy. And in the closing years of the nineteenth century its mines were struck by the Western Federation of Miners, leading to what one source called "a miniature war" characterized by "the terrorization of the local population by armed guards and deputies and the dynamiting of company property."

By the early 1970s, the bloody past was largely forgotten and, benefiting from a close-to-innocent atmosphere Stella Pence accurately recalls as "spontaneous, loose, and easy," the film festival became a success. So much of one, in fact, that all kinds of other celebrations, including events devoted to hot air balloons, bluegrass, wine, mushrooms, and chamber music, have made the town the de facto festival capital of the Rockies, a place busy enough to decide to schedule a "Nothing Festival" where "nothing happens all over town for this annual nonevent."

Beginning with Riefenstahl, Gloria Swanson, and Francis Ford Coppola that first year, Telluride initially attracted fans because of its one-of-a-kind in-person tributes in the Sheridan Opera House, which over time came to include almost every old and new cinema notable imaginable, from Hal Roach, Karl Struss, and Ben Carre to Harriet Andersson, Clint Eastwood, and Pedro Almodovar.

Starting, Bill Pence remembers, in the festival's eighth year, when *My Dinner with André* had its world premier at Telluride, the festival also became known for showing important new work. Films like *El Norte*,

Stranger Than Paradise, Paris, Texas, Blue Velvet, and *Babette's Feast* all benefited from having either their world or their North American premiers at the festival. Some films, like Michael Moore's *Roger and Me,* even came unsolicited, arriving over the transom on the last day of the selection process.

Because filmmakers heard tales of Telluride's intimate ambiance, they often came to experience it for themselves, leading to memorable personal moments like eighty-one-year-old Cab Calloway dancing across the Opera House stage and the ninety-year-old French director Abel Gance watching from his hotel window as his epic silent film *Napoleon* was projected on an outdoor screen.

No matter what you thought about Telluride, those personal moments were always indelible. In 1977, it was electrifying for me to have the still-vibrant and gracious silent star Viola Dana speak after a screening of *Blue Jeans,* a film she'd made sixty years earlier, and to hear meticulous British director Michael Powell, celebrated for *The Red Shoes, Black Narcissus,* and *Thief of Baghdad,* break down after a screening of the silent *Scaramouche,* made by his master, director Rex Ingram.

Originally scheduled only to talk before the film, Powell was so overcome by seeing *Scaramouche* again after so many years that he rose afterward and told the audience, very slowly and quite emotionally, that "it was from Rex Ingram that I learned standards. It cost me a great deal, but it's been worth it."

Twenty years later, I was equally moved by a similar cross-generational moment when French director and critic Bertrand Tavernier (*Round Midnight, A Sunday in the Country*) introduced *Remous,* a daring 1934 film dealing with such subjects as impotence, voyeurism, and sexual desire by the little-known Edmond T. Greville.

Tavernier talked passionately of being one of four young French film buffs who'd befriended Greville in 1960, of coming to admire and appreciate his work ("even his flaws are daring"). Finally, when the director died "alone and penniless," it was Tavernier and his friends who paid for the destitute man's funeral. Of such moments are Telluride memories made.

Because it is so small and particular, Telluride has also become known for its idiosyncrasies, like the long, long lines outside theaters, which one must join to ensure getting a seat at most programs. Also, after a local newspaper made more of a fuss on the eve of an early festival about a celebrated actress canceling for health reasons than about who was actually coming, Telluride has been zealous (and largely successful) about trying to keep its selections a secret until the night before screening begins.

Experiencing all this, critic Howie Movshowitz wrote in the *Denver Post*, is "like taking an unrest cure at some remote, half-crazy and incredibly effective sanatorium. You get no sleep, your eyes wind up sinking into your cheekbones, the films start to run together and you can hardly remember your name. But you're healed."

While the festival was universally admired and envied in its early years, this kind of fragrant praise gradually became sprinkled with the doubts of naysayers. Though it continued to sell out without difficulty, Telluride was increasingly faulted for its exclusivity and claustrophobia, called precious and "almost snobbish." There were mutterings, then *Los Angeles Times* film critic Sheila Benson reported, that it had become "smug, self-congratulatory, elitist." Even as steadfast a fan as critic Movshowitz noted that Telluride had "flirted with big star syndrome for a while."

After being overwhelmed by the third and fourth Telluride festivals, I wasn't able to return until the tenth, and to my chagrin I found the thrill somewhat gone. The event seemed more emotionally uneven, alternating between celebration and self-satisfaction, and the increasing intensity of the experience was not always what I wanted. By the time everything ended, with hundreds of cinema zealots crammed into the tiny Montrose, Colorado, airport batting opinions back and forth like beachballs as they waited for planes to Denver and beyond, I found I had to retreat to the peace and solitude of the parking lot to maintain what was left of my sanity. I didn't come back for ten years.

The Pences and Tom Luddy, while noting that they can be viewed as difficult ("We're not compromising, we don't make deals, maybe we can be a little bit too curt and honest," says Bill Pence), insist that at least from their point of view the festival's ambiance has never varied. And much of what has happened to Telluride could be attributed to the difficulties of an event gradually tripling in size as the town itself mushroomed as a ski resort and was able to accommodate increasing numbers of people. The idea that Telluride would ever be a place where a takeout spot called the Steaming Bean could sell more than 7,000 cups of coffee during the festival would have been inconceivable twenty-five years ago.

From a financial/logistical point of view, the Telluride festival has increasingly become what Bill Pence ruefully calls "a monster of its own creation." Perennially difficult and expensive to get to, Telluride is now so pricey a town that people who work in service jobs often have to live elsewhere, and the hotels, none of which existed when the festival started, now charge festival-goers what Stella Pence characterizes as "the highest of high season rates."

Festival prices, as noted, have also gone way up, a situation the Pences and Luddy agonize over, yet cannot help as long as the money from the sale of 1,300 tickets is needed to pay fully half of the event's cost. It's this desperate need for dollars to simply run the thing that has led to extensive and ever-increasing corporate sponsorship. The *Village Voice* journalist who was unnerved by the spectacle of a "Doc Martens' Southwestern Chili Chow Down" a few years back would marvel at the very visible support of Ralph Lauren and *Vanity Fair*, at a silent auction supervised by Sotheby's, and at a projected "Twenty-fifth Anniversary Special Theme Crossing" of the Queen Elizabeth II from New York to Southampton celebrating the festival.

The quest for funds is also behind the creation and persistence of high-end patron passes. Though their existence — and the right they confer to get admitted to theaters ahead of the milling crowds — have always blended awkwardly with Telluride's egalitarianism, the Pences defend these passes as essential to keeping the festival solvent and ticket prices for other attendees close to reasonable. "Patrons drive people crazy by getting in early, but those people are essentially subsidizing everyone else's ticket," says Stella Pence. "That money means general admission tickets don't have to go up."

The way Telluride's at times controversial nature dovetailed with my own qualms about the event made me a bit wary when I returned to town for the first time in a decade in 1993 for the fest's twentieth anniversary. What I found then was still true at the twenty-fifth: Telluride was a festival whose stubborn spirit and refusal to bend had helped it weather its storm. It's not that those problems had disappeared, but rather that they felt less important in the overall scheme of things.

With new festivals willing to show anything that moves erupting almost daily, and with established events like Toronto and Sundance getting bigger and increasingly attuned to the rhythms of the commercial marketplace, Telluride's rigor, its sense of standards, and its unquestioned love of film seem increasingly of value even if they're not to everyone's taste.

Another trend in the film world that Telluride counteracts is the gradual disappearance of what Bill Pence calls "the great independent specialty houses, the art theaters. There is an audience, albeit small, for specialized films that do not find a showcase." From cities across the country, the vanguard of that audience makes its way to Telluride and is important for creating word of mouth for unheralded films. "We never wanted to be an exclusive club of film buffs," says codirector Luddy. "We want people to go back home turned on about something they hadn't known about before. We wanted the festival to have a ripple effect."

As for the event's resilience, says Luddy, "Partly it's a question of timing; most festivals are too long, they become an ordeal." And most festivals do without Telluride's centerpiece, the old-fashioned Main Street, a National Historic Landmark District, which everyone gravitates to. "It's a proximity I really like, there's still a sense that everyone's together in the same summer camp," says Bill Pence. "No one else has that particular hothouse environment, the town really does become the festival. You can't build that artificially; it's either there or it isn't."

Yet, ever mercurial, no sooner does the Telluride Film Festival seem to be set in its ways than the potential for change becomes irresistible. Just days after extolling the virtues of having the town's radioactive core as a base, codirector Pence announced that the next edition of the festival would for the first time include programming at a theater in Mountain Village, reachable only by that gondola. "For our first twenty-five years, we've been one kind of festival," Pence said. "Maybe in our twenty-sixth year we'll start to become a somewhat different kind of festival." If it didn't have that kind of attitude, it just wouldn't be Telluride.

PART FOUR

The Politics of Festivals

The Festival That Failed

We are like Cyrano. We know we cannot win, but we fight.
We are a loser, but a faithful loser.
— *Daniel Toscan du Plantier,*
president, Unifrance Film International

ACAPULCO — It's hot here, jungle hot. Hibiscus and bougainvillea are flourishing and the sultry air seems almost perfumed. I'm alone at Las Brisas, a celebrated pink and white honeymoon spot with private swimming pools and spectacular views, feeling, to paraphrase Raymond Chandler's been-around Philip Marlowe, as out of place as a tarantula on a piece of angelfood cake. But it doesn't matter. Like Marlowe, I'm on a case.

The death of a film festival is what I'm investigating. That's right, in this boom time for fests, with unprecedented numbers thriving and new contenders clutching at life every day, one of them up and died. At least that's what some people say.

Others, and there are always others, mutter darkly that it was hardly a natural death. Sometimes they even pull you aside, look furtively over their shoulders, and insist the festival didn't really die at all. It's still alive, they tell you nervously, living in Mexico under another name, taking advantage of the cinematic equivalent of a witness protection plan. I knew I'd have to check this one out. Personally.

First, though, I hit the books, poring over parts of the dusty archives of what used to be the Sarasota French Film Festival, which for seven years (1989–1995) was a November adornment of a Florida Gulf Coast resort town described by *Time* as "a spot so chic and pretty it might have been transported whole from the Côte d'Azur."

Its aim, said critic Molly Haskell, the festival's artistic director, was "to increase the presence and revenue of French film in America." "It enabled," *Le Monde* added with appropriate grandeur, "a minnow (the French cinema) to swim for a few moments in pike-infested waters (the American movie industry) and escape not only unharmed but reinvigorated." And now it was floating belly up like yesterday's tuna.

Sarasota was, by all reports, one hell of a party while it lasted. I scanned lists in French of local clubs and restaurants prepared for the more than a hundred film notables who were flown in annually from France. I read notes about the dozens of American journalists who also attended ("not a beach person" was the inside word on one scribe) and examined itineraries for the American stars who came as well; it was all strictly legit. And then there were all those elaborate festival meals: Chateaubriand Automne, Patés à la Chinoise, Tranche de Roquet au Saffron. Talk about a condemned man eating a hearty meal.

Just as my research was about to hit caloric overload, I got a tip. Go to Acapulco in November. Ask for something called the Festival de Ciné Français. See if anything about it looks familiar. The phone went dead and I booked my flight.

Once I arrived, it wasn't only the honeymoon atmosphere of the festival headquarters hotel that was unsettling. Though the setting was Mexican, a good deal of public advertising was in English; billboards reading "Tony Roma's Famous for Ribs," "Hooters," and a picture of Colonel Sanders with the message "Visita Kentucky Hoy" crowded the highway in from the airport.

At the modern, 1,400-seat Juan Ruíz de Alarcon theater in the city's downtown convention center, my linguistic troubles took a different turn. Here were fifteen French films showing over four days, all with

Spanish subtitles. Not completely at home in either of those languages, with not a word of English in sight, I felt overmatched and uncertain how to proceed, but I didn't want to give up. The very emotions, it turned out, that helped me break The Case of the Fugitive Film Festival wide open.

You don't have to be a detective, of course, hard-boiled or otherwise, to understand the flip side of my Acapulco situation: as disoriented as I felt dealing with French films with Spanish subtitles, that's how confused and left out foreign films feel when they attempt to penetrate what to them is the baffling English-speaking American market. With the non-English language share of the U.S. box office consistently below 1 percent, a truly anorexic level, it's a crisis that affects film industries worldwide.

But while all countries have this problem, only the French refuse to accept the situation as a given. To fully understand why the Sarasota Film Festival lived, died, and was reborn in Acapulco, it's necessary to explore the singular attitude the French have to their current and past film heritage, to appreciate a way of looking at motion pictures that is both closely allied to American attitudes and completely divorced from them.

How seriously the French were taking the problem became apparent several years ago when Daniel Toscan du Plantier convened an elaborate lunch for key American film journalists at the Cannes Film Festival. The energetic Toscan, as he is universally known, is a successful producer (*Cousin, Cousine*, Bergman's *Fanny and Alexander*, Fellini's *City of Women*, among others) who for more than a decade has been the president of Unifrance, the entity charged with promoting French film overseas.

There was a time, as everyone around the table knew, when French film needed little help in this country. During the 1960s heyday of the *Nouvelle Vague*, the French New Wave, Americans became passionate about the work of directors like François Truffaut, Jean-Luc Godard, Alain Resnais, Louis Malle, Eric Rohmer, and Claude Chabrol. If you wanted to be considered film-literate or even just culturally sophisticated, these were pictures you had to see.

But while the French still have as many Best Foreign Language film nominations as any other country, plus the most Oscars, those days have vanished, not only for their pictures but also for all overseas product. Though there are periodic breakout films like *Cinema Paradiso, Life Is Beautiful,* and *Crouching Tiger, Hidden Dragon,* in general foreign films, as that anemic less than 1 percent of the market demonstrates, do not do the business or have the cachet that they once had. The audience was becoming so finite, Toscan joked, "that we've wondered, 'Why buy space for an ad in the *New York Times?* For the same money we could get a list of the people who go to our films and personally phone them all instead.'"

This situation is especially galling because of the powerful lock American films have on world markets in general, France included. More American films were released in France in 1997 than French-language films, and the United States captured a mammoth 55 percent of the French box office. In 1998, French films in France fell below 30 percent of the total audience, with only three French-made films listed among the top fifteen hits, a situation that the newspaper *Le Figaro* reported with a still from *Titanic* and the headline "Why French Cinema Is Sinking."

As discussed by the journalists around that lunch table in Cannes and revisited by Toscan in an extended interview during the Acapulco Festival, the reasons for the French fall from grace in the United States are numerous and interlocking. They range from broad societal changes like the ever-increasing competition for Americans' leisure time to specifics like the willingness of successful French directors (Luc Besson, Jean-Jacques Annaud, and, more recently, Mathieu Kassovitz) to forgo their native tongue and work on English-language projects. But all discussions inevitably come back to a trio of circumstances whose cumulative effect has been devastating.

(1) To put it as delicately as possibly, the core audience for French

films is aging into a time of life when moviegoing is not the passion it once was. "A coterie of middle-aged nostalgics" is how one writer unsympathetically described French film partisans, and Toscan himself once told the *Wall Street Journal* that "we need to go beyond that New York film type, the taxi driver wearing black reading Jean Renoir's biography in his spare time."

Though French director Bertrand Tavernier once complained about the inability of his country's films to break out of certain theaters and cities by claiming "we are kept on reservations like the Cherokee or the Navajo," those art houses and the elite press coverage that used to go with them are themselves an endangered species these days, making extended runs for foreign efforts increasingly problematic. "These films are not going to make it with the public based on thirty-second TV spots," says Michael Barker, cochairman of Sony Pictures Classics, one of the major distributors of French films in this country. "It hasn't happened before, and it won't happen now."

And while Toscan has characterized this situation by saying "French charm is obsolete," part of the difficulty is that the avatars of the latest generation of French directors, people like Arnaud Desplechin and Olivier Assayas, are influenced more by the astringent director Maurice Pialat (whose films like *A Nos Amours, Sous le Soleil de Satan,* and *Van Gogh* have never been popular in this country) than the empathetic Truffaut and are not very interested in being warm and cuddly. This theory is also Toscan's, who sums up by observing that "that special charm" is "no more the only definition of French cinema."

(2) As French cinema has changed, so has the new American movie audience, and for the worse. Most European audiences (except for the French, who, Toscan says, "are obsessed with original language, we have to be in the heart of authenticity") prefer to have their foreign films dubbed, but Americans have stubbornly and traditionally rejected that system. What is new is that these days, subtitles are getting just as rough a treatment.

"If you want to reach a large audience with a film, you cannot put subtitles on it," concedes Toscan, adding in mock exasperation, "Young people can read a computer screen, but for them the idea of reading a film is an impossible idea." One result is a frustrating situation where a Hollywood remake like *Three Men and a Baby* can earn approximately fifty times what the French original did in American business. No wonder critic Haskell, the former Sarasota artistic director, sums things up more in sorrow than anger, saying, "Americans have gotten spoiled and parochial."

(3) The audience that traditionally went to French films in the 1960s has been cannibalized by the explosive growth of the American independent movement. In decades past, to experience films that emphasized character, that were true to life and not mechanical and simplistic, to experience, in other words, an alternative to standard Hollywood product, foreign-language films were your only refuge.

But now, with independent film the hottest aspect of the American scene, audiences can get those same kinds of films without having to bother reading subtitles or hearing hollow dubbed voices. "Aside from artistic merit," adds Haskell, "in the days of the Production Code, French films had the merit of sensuality. The cachet of French cinema is that it was more adult, more sophisticated, more oo-la-la. It no longer is."

In the face of all these very substantial obstacles, other countries have to varying degrees given up on the possibility of their national cinemas making much of a dent in America's chauvinistic viewing habits. A trio of Italian cultural organizations recently started "Venezia a Hollywood," bringing five Italian films from the Venice Festival to Los Angeles, and the AFI in Washington hosts an annual European Union Film Showcase, but such efforts are few and far between, much to Toscan's discomfort. "It's my despair," he says, and he looks as though he means it.

The French, as Toscan noted, are different. Like Edmond Rostand's Cyrano de Bergerac, who persisted in loving the fair Roxanne though he knew she would never be his, the French have refused to give up on the prospects of their film industry, both at home and abroad. And that is, at least in part, because their attitude toward cinema is akin to our own.

"We have many things in common with the U.S., including taking film very seriously in terms of power," Toscan says. "We're the only countries where the presidents, both Bill Clinton and Jacques Chirac, think cinema is important enough to mention when they make state visits. We think the same; that's why we're fighting. The great empires think cinema is important. It's a kind of religion to both sides."

In addition, the French, who've made some of the world's greatest motion pictures in every decade of cinema's existence, feel, more self-consciously than Americans, that film is part of their heritage. "Cultural identity is a pretentious word in English, a heavy word, but it means something, and to French people film is one of the most important expressions of cultural identity," Toscan says. "It's not true in Italy, it's not true in Germany, it's not true in Mexico, but in France the heart of it, the best of it is the theatrical movie."

Not only, says Molly Haskell, do the French have "a sense of their own importance in movie history," they are "as moviegoers, scholars and appreciators generous in their attitude toward the rest of the world. So it's an offense to them that there's not any kind of reciprocity in the United States."

Jack Lang, France's former minister of culture and communications, echoed this sentiment when he told an interviewer, *à propos* France's determination to penetrate the U.S. market, "It's not so much a matter of making money. It's more a question of moral satisfaction. For a film to be shown in America amounts to a kind of international consecration for a foreign film maker." Added Toscan, when told by a U.S. trade representative that the film situation was the flip side of the cheese situation, that is, we eat theirs and they don't eat ours, "Our films are just as good as our cheese."

There are, obviously, elements of chauvinism in the French stance, what Haskell characterized as "a defiant attitude, a general irritation with American cinema as this kind of global juggernaut that's resented the same way they resented America going into Iraq." But along with that is the French feeling that more than being a nation-versus-nation situation, their position represents standing up for a different kind of cinematic tradition, the personal, individualistic works that in France are known as *films d'auteur.*

"If it's either big Hollywood or little France, we are dead," says Toscan, facing facts. "We cannot fight against American power; China and India aside, the U.S. controls 75 to 80 percent of the world's market. It's not America and France, it's Hollywood and the rest of the world, including America. It's not a war, it's an attempt to survive by the rest of the world, including American independents, young American film-makers who want to make small European films with no money. What we want to be are leaders of the alternative. What is good for cinema will surely be good for French cinema."

This is not just theoretical philosophizing. Because of that remarkable French consensus about the importance of films as part of national cultural identity, financing and taxation systems are in place that ensure ample funding for everything from modern theaters to the costs of production to the overseas activities of Unifrance.

Especially when compared to cultural funding in this country, where even traditional arts end up as beggars, the French largesse to film-related entities, which can amount to as much as $400 million per year (no, that's not a misprint) is more than impressive. It's not, Toscan explains, a line in the budget but rather a stream of revenue that flows from a series of stiff taxes, mostly on theatrical revenues. As a result, France supports close to two hundred film festivals and ranks behind only India and the United States in numbers of films made.

Also, because France, in Toscan's words, "chooses to defend cinema as culture against television as commerce," there are systems in place to ensure that the latter does not overrun the former. Television networks must invest 3 percent of their gross revenue in theatrical coproductions, and, even more against the American grain, network broadcasters aren't allowed to show films on Wednesday and Saturday nights, traditional French moviegoing evenings.

But, as people are wont to say in Los Angeles, there is money and there is Hollywood money. In 1997, the average cost of a studio film was $53 million plus, while the average French film cost $6.2 million. In addition, the studios regularly spend more to simply promote their films than the entire budgets of French efforts, which is why the French, determined to have an impact, have turned to creating their own festivals.

"If we had $50 million to open a film, we would not be making festivals, that is something for the poor," is how Toscan puts it. To help open Hollywood-dominated markets to their films, the French have started and supported thriving festivals in several nations (including Japan, Australia, Brazil, Hungary, and the Czech Republic), and it was in this spirit that the Sarasota French Film Festival began. It was a question, Toscan says, of "organizing our survival."

The notion of placing a festival in Sarasota came, however, not from the French but from the Floridians, specifically from a veteran politician named Robert M. Johnson. A Republican who represented Sarasota in the Florida state senate, Bob Johnson was able to gather pledges from business interests as well as a financial commitment from the state legislature that ended up being worth $250,000 a year for the festival's first five years.

"Bob came to Paris with a delegation of eight old and rich ladies from Florida, and we were so surprised, no one wanted to receive them," Toscan remembers. "We'd never heard the name Sarasota, it meant nothing to us, but on the other hand in my life I'd never heard of public money in America being dedicated to cinema."

Once they got to know Sarasota and the Sarasotans, the French increasingly warmed to the idea of a festival in a wealthy beachfront community that was considered a cultural oasis and was home to a well-known art museum founded by circus magnate John Ringling.

"What we love is a nice place, a seaside to convince our film colleagues to come with us," Toscan explains. "Sarasota turned out to be a charming place, with charming people. There was a museum with great paintings, an opera house, and Ringling's son had been one of the husbands of Martine Carol. We said, 'Why don't we try?'"

The French also liked the idea of Sarasota because it offered a chance for them to display their films to potential distributors in the best possible way. "In New York, professionals look at movies in small rooms with three phones, the life of a movie is suspended on the caprice of a very few people," Toscan explained. "Here we would invite New York distributors and critics to see films in a real theater [the Asolo Center for the Performing Arts] with a real audience. Not specialists or film buffs, but nice people discovering movies they'd never heard of. Buyers are influenced by a good reception in a full theater. It's a better way to sell."

With the help of a luminary-heavy honorary committee (including Louis Malle, Douglas Fairbanks Jr., Norman Mailer, and Elie Wiesel, among others), the Sarasota festival became a reality in 1989, and at first everyone seemed to be happy.

Under artistic director Haskell, a self-described "passionate Francophile," the festival programmed the cream of French cinema, including eventual Oscar winners *Indochine* and *Burnt by the Sun* (a French coproduction). The *Miami Herald* generously proclaimed Sarasota "Florida's best pure film festival," the *New York Times* called it one of the world's up and coming events, and headlines like "19 Frenchies For Florida Fest" became common in newspapers nationwide.

The festival was also good for relations between France and Sarasota in particular ("une petite ville charmante," *France-Soir* gushed) and Florida in general. French flags appeared in windows of Sarasota shopping malls, the city achieved a name recognition in France exceeded only by Miami and Orlando among Florida metropolises, and, it was repeatedly reported, Tropicana products spiked upward in France after the festival's inauguration.

Increased orange juice sales, however, did not captivate all the people all the time, and the Sarasota Festival almost immediately faced obstacles. There were disputes about how many tickets were given away versus the number sold, run-ins with an irate local art house programmer who felt disrespected, and, perhaps inevitably, there were persistent cultural clashes.

The French were irked when *Sarasota Magazine* listed "Ten Commandments" for those wishing to become French ("marry and get yourself a mistress," "feel superior," "believe that Jerry Lewis is really, really funny"). And Sarasotans were not amused when a correspondent for *Le Figaro* wrote, "In Sarasota, only the pelicans — gorged and dirty — possess vitality."

The most long-lived and ultimately most damaging criticism had to do with the government money spent, money that, absent an American tradition of public funding for the arts, numerous local residents could not reconcile themselves to.

Molly Haskell, who remembers "a certain provincialism on the part of Sarasota," recalled comments that Senator Johnson had spent "$500,000 of Florida money so he could have lunch with Catherine Deneuve." And an irate local letter-to-the-editor writer demanded to know "what has happened to our sense of value? The French Film Festival is a pretense at high culture. . . . The dinners and receptions are aglitter in evening gowns and diamonds. Neither the films nor the receptions are of interest to the great majority of Floridians."

It was the charges against Johnson that most resonated with local voters. They surfaced in the 1992 Republican primary, when Johnson's opponent ridiculed the festival as a "pork barrel project." Johnson fought off that challenge, but despite his sixteen years in office, he was defeated in November by Democrat Jim Boczar, who made the festival the centerpiece of his campaign. Running, according to *Variety*, "on an austerity platform in this recession-hit region, his campaign oratory made frequent reference to the lavish festival as a boondoggle that cost Florida taxpayers $1 million."

With its main local champion vanquished, it was only a matter of time until the French pulled the plug on Sarasota, which, for a variety of reasons, they did in June 1996. The attacks on the festival in those political campaigns didn't endear the state to the French ("They were hostile, incredibly provincial in a bad sense," Toscan says), and the financial situation was also not promising. "It was a costly festival, we lost the subsidy of Florida, there was no more support from anyone, and if we do not have private sponsorship, we must leave," Toscan explains. "We said, 'It is enough. We are fed up with Sarasota, we must find another place.'"

As Haskell points out, there was also another reason to leave Sarasota. The French, always looking to the future, were not completely happy with the audience they were getting. "It wasn't young enough," Haskell reports. "They wanted new, wider, younger audiences, and what they were getting were Francophiles, French professors, scholarly types and the national membership of the Alliance Française." Toscan agrees: "In a way we were glad to leave Florida. It was not a place for young people but for old ladies speaking about Truffaut."

Though the festival concept did not work in Sarasota, the French have by no means given up on the United States as a market for their films. Toscan has all kinds of schemes afoot, from hosting several smaller festivals to possibly supporting French films once they are released out of a special fund for prints and advertising. "The U.S. market is essential to us," he says, "but very difficult."

Neither have the French given up on the festival concept as the best way to get their films wider exposure and distribution around the world; given their zeal for the cinema, there is no way they could. Which is how the Sarasota French Film Festival moved south, took advantage of government subsidies, and became Acapulco's Festival de Ciné Français, which annually plays host to journalists, distributors, and exhibitors from Argentina, Brazil, Chile, Colombia, Cuba, Peru, Uruguay, and Venezuela (as well as, of course, Mexico), in sum a sizable potential market.

Things were not always this bright. When the French were considering Acapulco as a festival site, Toscan visited with director and cinephile Tavernier. "We went to a school classroom and asked 'have any of you heard of French cinema?' and the answer was 'no,'" he remembers. "In desperation, Bertrand asked if anyone had seen a French film, and a boy in the back raised his hand. 'My father spoke about a French film,' he said. 'It was called *Emmanuelle*.'"

Despite this unpromising beginning, Acapulco, where young people in fact make up a healthy proportion of the audience, is turning into a genuine beachhead for French cinema. Congenitally upbeat, Toscan is delighted. The future here and elsewhere, if he has anything to do with it, will have a distinctly French accent.

"If you are on a street full of hamburger shops, you finally want to eat something else," Toscan sums up, brimming with passion. "If you hear there is an old lady who prepares *cassoulet* in a small apartment on the second floor, you will go there, you will seek her out. In a film world where there is too much noise, too much *Independence Day*, French cinema is *cassoulet* on the second floor."

I, the Jury

He was all eagerness and animation, this young man deep in conversation in a hotel lobby. "The aesthetics of these films are so different," he insisted to his friends, eyes hot with emotion. "I can't imagine being on the jury at this festival."

I had to smile as I walked past, not only because the speaker reminded me of myself a couple of decades back, but also because I happened to be one of the seven members of the jury at the twentieth Montreal World Film Festival. And in fact the state of affairs was as the young man imagined, a situation hard to visualize in the abstract that became more surprising, more exhausting, and more gratifying than almost any cinematic experience I could remember.

It was because the work of juries was so closed off and unknowable to outsiders that I'd been curious to participate for almost as long as I'd realized the position existed. My interest in juries as forces for good intensified after Cannes in 1993 when the chairman, French director Louis Malle, engineered the decision most people wanted but dared not dream of: a rare splitting of the Palme d'Or between Jane Campion's *The Piano* and Chen Kiage's *Farewell My Concubine*.

Understandably pleased with what he had accomplished, Malle came over to chat with a group of American journalists at the closing night party. "I'm as proud of having done this," he said, satisfaction all over his face, "as anything in my career."

Of course, through the years I'd heard all kinds of other stories about how these panels operated, juicer tales that made jury life seem well suited for a series on the Fox Network. Rumors of backbiting, rivalries, and jealousy were everywhere, as were festivals where the films hadn't shown up, where jurors needed bodyguards or played tennis instead of seeing the movies, where a juror had insisted on taking her unruly cat to all the screenings, only to have it invariably escape and disrupt the theater.

Sometimes factionalism on juries had become so extreme that a film won because both sides detested it equally. Berlin before the Communists fell, with its wall dividing the city between the West and the Soviet bloc, had been a natural setting for divisiveness. One jury member remembered a Russian actress who announced, before a single film had been screened, that voting for anything from the United States or Canada was out of the question for her.

Especially good for trouble was the anarchic German director Rainer Werner Fassbinder. Once, in a particularly provocative mood, he determined what the worst film in the Berlin competition was and insisted it win the Golden Bear, reducing an American actress on the jury to tears of frustration and rage.

Perhaps my favorite jury tale came from Donald Ritchie, the doyen of Western writers on Japanese film, who described how you indicate preference in a country where expressing strong opinions is frowned on. "First everyone around the table mentions all the entries and agrees 'these are all good films.' On the second round, you do the same thing and, if there is a film you favor, you name it at the end and say 'this, this also is a good film.'"

Since the kind of jury experience I'd have would depend on my fellow panel members, all chosen by festival head Serge Losique, I was naturally curious as to who they were. The renowned French actress Jeanne Moreau was to be the chairman, to be joined by another award-winning actress, Spain's Assumpta Serna, and a former critic, Guglielmo Biraghi from Italy, who'd also run both the Taormina and Venice festivals in his country.

Two members were directors: Cuba's Humberto Solás, whose *Lucia* was a classic of Latin American cinema, and Hungary's Judit Elek, whose *To Speak the Unspeakable — The Message of Elie Wiesel* had just been well received at Cannes. Finally there was French Canadian producer Denis Heroux, with films like *Atlantic City* and *Quest for Fire* to his credit.

It was an impressive group. Maybe even too impressive. Suddenly I realized I was the only native English speaker on the entire panel. How would we communicate, I wondered, and other worries, each more irrational than the last, soon followed.

Would I be faced with a cabal of aesthetic zealots whose taste would run to the obscure and unwatchable? Would I in reaction turn into the worst kind of American chauvinist, insisting on the plastic qualities of Sylvester Stallone's work? Would I get a late-night phone call from Jack Valenti, pleading with me to stand by the flag? Clearly this jury business might be more complicated than I thought.

Although Montreal is one of the world's larger film festivals, showing hundreds of films over its twelve-day span, only twenty-one of those would be in the official competition, and when I got a look at the list of titles, a completely different set of concerns made themselves known.

While the competition films came from sixteen countries (including Albania, India, Iran, Israel, Romania, Sweden, and South Korea), most of them were unknown to me, made by directors I was unfamiliar with, or both. What if the unthinkable happened and I couldn't find anything to get passionate about? Or what if everyone loved everything I hated, and vice versa? Would I be subject to cutting remarks in obscure languages? Or worse?

Once I arrived in Montreal and made my way through the hefty 400-page official program, I began to realize that the festival's international quality, both in and out of competition, was the essence of its identity. It is also critical to how the World Film Festival defines itself in relation to its rival some three hundred miles down Highway 401, the Toronto International Film Festival.

Though their dates are close (Toronto began three days after Montreal ended) and they often try to snare the same films, the festivals say they don't really compete with each other, and while that sounds like a publicity nostrum, the claim contains a core of truth. Near as they are geographically, Montreal and Toronto can be seen as representing opposite poles of today's film world.

Toronto shows its share of obscure and worthwhile films, but its ethos, the reason for its success, is that it's the place to go if you want to be the first on your block to see what's going to be hot in the upcoming fall season. And as the movie business changed and it became clear that lucrative acquisition deals could be made on smaller pictures, Toronto became the North American equivalent of Cannes, the place where films are seen, the heat created, and the handshakes given.

Even French Canadian films made in the province of Quebec, like Robert Lepage's *Le Confessional* and Jean-Claude Lauzon's *Leolo*, films that should have been naturals for Montreal, premiered at Toronto's event for commercial reasons. As Piers Handling, director of the Toronto Festival, told *Maclean's*, the Canadian news magazine, his city is "friendly, safe and anglophone. The Americans don't feel like they are going to a foreign city, which is important to them."

Montreal, by contrast, exists to show films that not only won't get hot but also may in fact never be so much as seen elsewhere. Serge Losique, who founded the event, wrote in the program that "the Festival has become an obligatory dose of oxygen for those who are interested in what is being made in foreign cinemas." Says French actor Gérard Depardieu, who visited in 1995, "It's what I call Cinema Planet." For cinephiles like director Brian De Palma, who comes most years to sample the wide selection, no other festival can replace its breadth and noncommercial environment.

In some ways typical of Montreal fare (though paradoxically scheduled for Toronto as well), was something called *Seven Servants*, a hopelessly absurd film starring Anthony Quinn as a caftan-clad tycoon searching for meaning in his life. He pays a man $10,000 to put a finger in his ear and keep it there twenty-four hours a day for ten days. Then he pays another man to do the same for the other ear, a third man to do likewise for one nostril, a forth for the second. Most of the film consists of these five people moving in tandem across lawns and floors like some enormous crab. Really.

This international mix has been extremely popular with Montreal's citizens (annual attendance in the 400,000 range allows the event to call itself the largest publicly attended film festival in the Western world). More than that, it seems fair to speculate that on a psychological level the city probably had no choice but to host an event like this.

Montreal is a bilingual metropolis in the only Canadian province with a francophone majority, and its obsession with what the local French press calls "la crise linguistique" reaches a level of intensity difficult for outsiders to credit. So this city's festival could no more bend over backward to make English speakers feel at home than Toronto's could insist on Chinese subtitles for all its films.

Like many of the world's intractable crises, the battle between English and French in Montreal and Quebec has a long and complex history. Concerned that French is disappearing under the inexorable tide of worldwide English hegemony, the province's ruling Parti Québecois has pushed through a series of laws to redress the balance, like one that says all English commercial signs must be either half the size or half as numerous as their French counterparts.

(Sometimes this determination to protect national character can go to extreme lengths. In an episode the local press called "Matzogate," kosher for Passover products imported from the United States with English-only labels were pulled from Quebec shelves only two weeks before the holiday. When a compromise was reached between the government and the Jewish community, the *Gazette*, the city's only English-language newspaper, made "Passover Products Cleared" the four-column banner across the top of page one.)

Ever since a province-wide referendum on the possibility of independence for Quebec ended in almost a dead heat (everyone in the city
knows the 50.6 percent "no" versus 49.4 percent "yes" figures), the situation has gotten, if possible, worse, with a new militancy on the part of
English speakers leading to newspaper headlines about "the summer of
the angry anglo."

One of the results of these internecine battles is a film festival that has
been called more determinedly French than Cannes. When director
Lina Wertmüller, admitting that her English was abominable and her
French a disgrace, asked the audience which language she should use to
introduce her film, all the voices boomed "française." Said one journalist, upset about the increasing number of French films shown without
English subtitles, "I've been coming here for twenty years and the siege
mentality gets worse and worse."

Aside from its determination to stay international and not become
what scoffers call "a dog and pony show for Hollywood," what sets
Montreal apart from Toronto and gives it a distinctive character is that
it's the only Class A competitive film festival in North America recognized by the International Federation of Film Producers Association,
putting it on a par with the European big four of Cannes, Berlin, Venice,
and Moscow. Which is where we the jury rejoin the picture.

Their resumes notwithstanding, the jurors turned out to be a genial
and good-humored bunch, constitutionally averse to taking themselves
too seriously. On the average each member had been on half a dozen
panels (Guglielmo Biraghi had been on that many in a single year), and
it was a source of some amusement to find what one of them called "a
jury virgin" in their midst.

The chairman, Jeanne Moreau, had previously headed juries in
Cannes, Berlin, New Delhi, Avoriaz, and Monte Carlo. At once spontaneous, conscientious, and playful (novelist Nadine Gordimer, a fellow
judge at Cannes, called her personality "an unlikely combination, at
once imperious and lovable"), Moreau set an admirable tone for the proceedings. "Judging isn't protecting yourself from emotion," she said at a

press conference. "How can you approach a film coldly? You have to open up and be ready to receive. Cinema is the mirror of the world."

Judging soon settled into a soothing routine. Each morning the seven of us would rendezvous at the lovely circa 1912 Cinema Imperial for a double bill that began at nine and was broken in half by a coffee break at an adjoining festival office. Not only did we always sit in the same blocked off row, such was the force of habit that we ended up almost always occupying the same seats.

Because gossiping to outsiders about what we liked or disliked is understandably forbidden, being on a jury encourages a sense of removal from the rest of the festival. Not for us was dishing the hot films or keeping tabs on what everyone was saying, both critical to the life of a working journalist. Locked into a kind of monastic seclusion, we became dependent on each other for companionship and stimulation.

That traveling-in-a-bubble factor creates one of the most satisfying aspects of jury life, the sense of bonding among members that begins, probably in much the way it did for the O.J. Simpson jurors, in a camaraderie of misery.

For while it's a given of festival life that walking out on endless, pointless, and uninvolving films is not only permissible but also essential to maintain a semblance of mental health, if you are on a jury you absolutely, positively cannot leave. As we suffered together through films that were tedious beyond belief, we identified strongly with each other, not to mention a character in one competition film who screamed "Art takes sacrifice" as a group of prostitutes emptied chamber pots on his head. Sacrifice indeed.

Part of the reason journalists and audience members can leave but we couldn't is because what a jury does matters. Reviews and public cheers and hisses come and go, but awards last and often have a considerable impact on the success of the films in competition as well as the careers of people who make them.

This was something everyone in our group implicitly understood. We were serious, we were professional, and we worked so assiduously that we may have been the first jury in Montreal history to spend considerably more time in meetings than at parties.

While some juries get together only once, to take a final vote, the seven of us met for hours-long sessions every other day. Because Moreau did not want anyone to experience frustration at being unheard, we discussed each film at length, thoroughly airing our likes and dislikes, pulling apart and dissecting what we loved as well as what we didn't.

Familiar with the acrimony that can attend similar discussions at critics' organizations, I was impressed by the intelligence and tolerance of the group and how willing everyone was to acknowledge flaws in their favorites and tolerate unfamiliar opinions. As jurors sipped cups of black coffee and talked through clouds of cigarette smoke about life, literature, the theater, and film, our meetings resembled those vivid Parisian cafe conversations that were a staple of the classic French New Wave films of the 1960s.

Enhancing that sensation was the fact that the discussions, excursions into both Spanish and English notwithstanding, were often in the language the jury as a whole was most comfortable in, which turned out to be French. Yes, everyone understood English and was happy enough to translate what I didn't understand, and, yes, this kind of immersion experience markedly improved my comprehension during the course of the festival. But still it was disheartening to represent American parochialism by being the only juror who wasn't bilingual at the very least.

When it came time for the jury's final meeting, the thoroughness of our previous sessions paid considerable dividends. Not only had we already eliminated many of the least worthy contenders, but also we'd gained a respect for each other's opinions that mitigated against the kind of going-down-with-the-ship fanaticism that had doomed other juries to deliberations that lasted till early in the morning.

Instead, within the space of a couple of hours, we very smoothly allocated the seven awards (plus two for shorts) within our power. Because none of the twenty-one features turned out to be a life-changing masterpiece that insisted on its preeminence, we were faced instead with the task of distributing the awards in a sensible manner among the films that we felt were strongest.

The top prize, the augustly named Grand Prix of the Americas, went to a British film, *Different for Girls*, that convincingly brought the conventions of romantic comedy to the rarely seen world of transsexuals. The film had its problems, but the core relationship, impeccably acted by Steven Macintosh and Rupert Graves, was everything it should be.

In our most Solomonic move, we split the festival's runner-up award, the Special Grand Prix of the Jury, between two very different films. *Un Air de Famille*, directed by France's Cedric Klapisch, was a hilarious, perfectly pitched black comedy about a feuding family that also won the People's Choice Award as the festival's most popular film. It shared the jury prize with an elusive, elliptical, beautifully shot Japanese film called *Sleeping Man*, a small work that charmed us with its determination to be, as one jury member put it, "off-, off-, one hundred times off-Broadway."

That final meeting, and the satisfaction we all took in being as fair as we could, underlined what I came to appreciate most about jury service. It was the rare sense of being part of a community that believes in film, that cares deeply enough about the medium to put in the effort necessary to reward good work. So much of the film business, for actors, writers, directors, and producers as well as for critics, is frustrating and adversarial that having the opportunity to work closely together for the common good was more gratifying than I could have imagined.

Several hours after the public awards ceremony, as I was headed out for a late-night bagel run (Montreal has the world's best), I found myself alone in an elevator with of the filmmakers involved with *Sleeping Man*. He looked at me and gravely said, "Thank you. It is a great honor. We did not expect it."

Louis Malle, I think, would have understood how I felt.

Compositor: BookMatters, Berkeley
Text: 10/15 Adobe Janson
Display: Adobe Janson
Printer and Binder: Friesens